C3

JAPANESE RAINMAKING

'Pine-meeting'; part of the preparation of New Year decorations

JAPANESE
RAINMAKING

and Other Folk Practices

GEOFFREY BOWNAS

with line drawings by
Pauline Brown

London
GEORGE ALLEN & UNWIN LTD
RUSKIN HOUSE   MUSEUM STREET

FIRST PUBLISHED IN 1963

PRINTED IN GREAT BRITAIN
in 13 pt Perpetua type
BY SIMSON SHAND LTD
LONDON, HERTFORD AND HARLOW

In memory of
YANAGIDA KUNIO
1875-1962

Preface

Anyone who reads Japanese will soon be aware of the immense debt I owe in this study of aspects of Japanese folk practices to Yanagida Kunio, the Institute he founded and the work he inspired. He was ever ready to discuss and to assist both in broad outline and fine detail: he had a truly remarkable knowledge of the bibliography of and the specialists in his subject and he would introduce you to both with an infectious eagerness. While fully acknowledging its unworthiness and inadequacies, I dedicate this work to Professor Yanagida's memory in token of this debt.

I must thank the Leverhulme Trust, the Spalding Trust and Tenri University for generous assistance which made possible the two periods of study in Japan during which material was gathered. I was able to see the rainmaking practices at Iwashimizu and the Bon dance at Shinjō thanks to the vigilant help of teachers at Tenri and the local press. Although too many Japanese scholars gave unstintingly of their time and knowledge for me to be able to name them one by one, it would be ungracious not to mention Suzuki Osamu of the Tenri Library, Hashimoto Tetsuo and Miyahata Mineo of Shiga University. The material for Chapter Nine, The Village Year, was gathered in the course of a sociological survey of three communities in Shiga Prefecture. I am indebted to the BBC for permission to reproduce parts of this material from a Third Programme feature.
Oxford 1963

Contents

One

INTRODUCTION

There are many indications that the Japanese are a racial amalgam, the major constituents arriving both from the west, over the northern mainland of Asia, and from the south, by way either of the Pacific islands or the south-eastern fringes of China. The Japanese language itself affords a good example of this diversity of origin. It has certain structural affinities with Korean and with other members of the Ural-Altaic group. One influence of such links is to be found in the phenomenon of vowel harmony—the appearance of only one of the vowels within a given word, even to the point of variation in a suffix vowel to retain symmetry with that of the word to which it is attached. Another pointer to the Ural-Altaic kinship of Japanese lies in the nature of its number words; the root of the word for 'five', as in Mongolian and Manchurian, is related to that for 'to close', the roots of the word for 'ten' and of 'open' are identical—and as he counts on the fingers of one hand, the Japanese closes down from one to five, so that the fist is clenched on five, then he opens up one finger each for six to ten, ending with an open and extended palm.

Yet, although these and other structural parallels occur, there has been little vocabulary borrowing from this linguistic group. On the other hand, the peoples of the Pacific, the second main component of the Japanese racial make-up, while they have worked little or no influence on the structural features of the language, have yet given it many of their words. Vocabulary identities exist between Japanese and, among others, Formosan, Annamese, Tagalog, Malay and the language of Munda. These, of themselves and unsupported by structural or grammatical parallels, prove little more than that the Japanese have long been good borrowers; it was an old-established trait that led them in the sixteenth century to adopt from the Portuguese *pan* and *kasuteira* for bread and castella—a kind of sponge-cake—and in the twentieth, to incorporate a host of words from all over Europe and the Americas. Nor does the Japanese word-hunter simply borrow; he distorts—to suit his physical and vocal limitations, a weak lower lip for example—he abbreviates and cross-breeds with his loan-words to father linguistic mongrels of the kind of *aru-saro*—which stands for 'arbeit salon', the poor man's night club where the needy student arbeits to provide her tuition fees.

There is other evidence for the South Sea contribution to the Japanese racial composition. Many of the books of the 'Spirit of the Japanese Nation' type, written in English around the turn of the century by Japanese who had visited or received an education from the West, point to two basic physical patterns; the one, the northern stream, has the noble face, the lighter skin and the high angular nose of the so-called 'princely' Mongol stock, the other has the dark pigment, the flattened nose and the broad lips of the man born near the equator. And where, in the linguistic field, the northerner appears to have triumphed, in many cultural aspects it is the influence of the southerner that is still the stronger. The Japanese architect, for example, except of course for the designer of the twentieth century department store and office block, has never quite come to terms with the chill of the snow and the winter winds of this new northern home, although his planning is ideally matched to the sticky heat of the Japanese summer. And though, like the Englishman, the Japanese will often use a comment on the weather to start up a conversation, you hear the exclamation 'Isn't it cold?' in winter far more often than the Englishman's heatwave greeting, 'Isn't it hot?'

Again, in matters that are the subject of this inquiry, the concept of the deity, origin myths, folk practices and so on, there are frequent approximations between the Japanese and the Polynesian. This is not to claim racial affinity (as the Japanese have often done) on the score merely of such meagre analogous occurrence or development; the student of cultural history—for want of a better term, though the Japanese fondness for it renders it eminently appropriate here—is confronted by too many such parallels, occurring often almost simultaneously at opposite ends of the world, to conclude other than that there is and has been a deal of haphazard and unrelated convergence.

The culture and manners of this racial amalgam are often the outgrowth of a wide-ranging eclecticism. Yet the products of the borrowing to which this eclecticism has led are only rarely allowed to escape the thoughtful and modifying attention of the borrower. Until modern times it was the Chinese cultural bank (and its Korean branches) that was almost always the chief creditor, and only rarely in Japan's history, under an intensely nationalistic and isolationist regime, has the charge of un-Japanese activities been levelled against such as imprudently displayed zeal for or erudition in matters Chinese. For the rest, offering precious little in return (the list of her cultural exports to China contains cormorant fishing, the rickshaw and not much more) Japan has usually acted as an avid assimilator of just about everything that found its way either up to China from India and thence to Japan, or direct from China or—and sometimes already in a stamp other than the original—from China by way of Korea. Japan's islands, lying off the east coast of the Asiatic mainland, were the final staging point in the eastward or north-eastern movement of cultural development, in much the same way as England, off the coast of Europe in the direction of the main flow of the Mediterranean cradle cultures, often constituted the final resting point in the journey of once new and exciting discoveries. Thus Japan became, in many aspects, the antique shop of the Orient, finding room for and obliged to accept—as often happens with the antique dealer—much that was already outmoded or quite inappropriate to its new surroundings.

Yet it was just this eagerness to adopt anything and everything on offer that made of Japan the treasure-house of the Orient; and the hoard was enriched in no small degree by the almost museum-type mentality of the Japanese, a trait still very apparent today. I have lived for two years in a newly-built Japanese house and never once sat on a settee stripped of its dust covers in my 'western style' room (complete with mantelpiece but lacking chimney-stack), never once been allowed to pollute with my foreigner's gaze the exquisite (or so I was assured by my landlord) black lacquer lining the alcove in the first-floor Japanese room. There are many priceless relics in Japan's Pan-Oriental treasure vaults; only there can you hear today a performance of *gagaku*—'elegant music'—which derives very closely from and has preserved all the elements of the music of the T'ang Court; and there is a number of Confucian temples in provincial cities as well as in Tokyo where the ritual of the service is not very different from that detailed in Chinese records of the Ming period.

But let it not be imagined that a knowledge, however broad it be, of things Chinese offers of itself free and automatic entry to this Japanese repository. There are many hindrances to such inter-availability of knowledge. First and foremost, for example, there is the language bar. Agreed, Japanese and Chinese characters are identical, for Japan borrowed to enable, in the first place, the keeping of records. There was no previous system of writing in Japan— there cannot have been, for any earlier or indigenous method must have been better suited to its purpose, as anyone will tell you who has been obliged to struggle with the distortions and the makeshift devices to which the Japanese have been obliged to resort to render this alien vehicle in any way roadworthy. Chinese and Japanese may be written in identical characters, but here all resemblance ceases; linguistic structure, syntax, grammar, division by parts of speech, conjugational aids and so on, all are radically different. The average Chinese university graduate will barely make sense of a passage of Japanese, and the Japanese scholar today, robbed since the war of his 'O' Level grammar school Chinese, lacks many of the keys that fit the door to his ancestral inheritance in much the same way that the Latin-less Oxford matriculant is allegedly bereft of the capacity to develop into the compleat gentleman.

It has been the fashion in Japan and China, as well as in the West, to pay little serious regard to, if not openly to deride, this so-called pale reflection of the Chinese original that is to be had in Japan. Ueno Museum in Tokyo has three vast galleries of bronze mirrors; the first is Chinese, the second displays Korean products; and that is where the average museum-goer stops and retraces his steps. My guide halted and hesitated at the threshold of the third gallery: 'The rest were "made in Japan",' he explained and, with a deprecatory shrug of the shoulders when confronted by this distasteful and inferior home-produce, he was for whisking me off to Chinese pots until, forced to turn and enter, he grudgingly admitted that Japan-made mirrors were not so shoddy after all.

In spite of Japan's intense pride in the uniqueness of her civilization (the use of the word *koku*—'national', 'of our glorious nation'—as a prefix to terms like 'studies', 'history' and 'language' testifies to this pride) until about the start of this century the best of her linguists, historians and so on have almost always been channelled into the paddy of Chinese studies. It is only with the advent of and the accordance of recognition to scholars in home fields of the calibre of Yanagida Kunio and Origuchi Nobuo (and, more recently, as a result of the gradual growth in inaccessibility of the Asiatic mainland) that there has arisen a group of disciplined schools of Japanese studying Japan. In such circumstances, the old prejudices die hard. If some aspect of Japanese culture bears the external marks of Buddhist, say, or Chinese origin or influence, in many cases that is held to be the end of the matter; research is jettisoned, scrutiny withheld, the Buddhist or Chinese prototype is described in detail and its Japanese imitation briefly analysed in relation to the supposed original. This is a feature, for example, of many of the

loose and inadequate discussions by Japanese of the ceremonies of Bon, centred round the fifteenth of the seventh
month. An arguable Chinese parallel exists, and it is snapped
up forthwith as the genuine prototype. Then, the picture is
rounded off by citation of a series of records and directives
relating to the Japanese Court. Little place is given to a
comparative analysis of the rituals of Bon and the 'Little New
Year'; the latter is celebrated with its central ceremonies

New Year Mummers

falling on the fifteenth of the first month and the two thus
divide the year into half, proving to be, in fact, the main
events of many in the Japanese festival year that occur on the
fifteenth day, that of the full moon by the old lunar calendar.

The same is true of many studies by Japanese of the element
of the race or contest to be found in a number of ritual
practices. The Chinese of the south fought out races in long

boats equipped with many paddles; so did, and do, the Japanese, particularly those of Kyūshū whose western seaboard is more close to China than any other stretch of Japan's long coastline. Ergo, boat races and any other ceremonies in the nature of a contest are best and most adequately interpreted as direct imitations of the Chinese practice. But look more closely and you find the contest (between fires, boats; a tug of war and so on) in the mountain farming village as well as on the western shores of Kyūshū; you find it more particularly at Bon and at New Year—the two great dividing points in the year when the farmer thinks ahead and wonders how his crops will fare in the period to come—and the contest is, in part, a mode of divination, its outcome an indication of the spirits' will and plan.

It is clear then that for a competent understanding of many of Japan's folk customs, however much they may appear superficially to be a valuable living replica of a Chinese prototype no longer practised or, if still in existence, unrecognizably distorted, one must work down below the Chinese veneer to an indigenous canvas. The distinction between Shintō and Buddhism may often serve as a rudimentary criterion to distil the indigenous from the foreign, for, although the two great religions of Japan quickly merged and, during a thousand years of not unfriendly inter-borrowing, created a 'Dual Shintō' which owed much to Buddhism, yet from the seventeenth century onwards there was in certain orthodox yet vigorous Shintō priestly circles a lively attempt to rid the indigenous faith of its alien trappings. However, while many of the folk practices described later do, in fact, come under the protection of Shintō interpreted in its widest sense, this demarcation based on Shintō and Buddhism is, at best, a rough one. The Japanese farmer, if made to stop and think, would no doubt describe the Bon ceremonies of his village as Buddhist; he would most certainly also attribute to Buddhism most of his actions as a participant in funeral ritual: but, as we shall see, there are numerous aspects of either of these which are not Buddhist in origin.

Demon-driving fires are lit on the night of the full moon in the first and seventh months

Introduction

Again, by and large, Buddhism is of greater account to the individual and Shintō of greater significance to the social group, the mountain hamlet or the small urban collocation. Since most of the folk practices I shall examine are those of the group, we shall be dealing more with ceremonies ascribed to Shintō and practised by Shintō officials or at Shintō foundations.

But now we should pause to define terms. Shintō means, literally, the 'Way of the Spirits'. But the connotation of this 'Way of the Spirits' varies drastically with its context. Tied to the coat-tails of nationalistic fervour, as in the 'thirties and early 'forties, Shintō's cosmological doctrines became, for many, infallible evidence not only for the divinity and primacy of the Emperor through his direct descent from the Sun Goddess, but also for the unique and invincible qualities of his subjects in virtue of their relationship, as his children, to the Emperor. A national religion, founded not on a canon but on conveniently handy eighth century historical docu-ments (which contained a generous admixture of early myths and primitive cosmological notions) became the foundation of political theory and dogma; the Emperor's position, thus bolstered, was to be subject not even to the analysis of the political theorist, much less to the criticism of any daring opposition spokesman. As such, Shintō became one of the principal targets for suppression and reform during the years of the American occupation. But, through their aversion to precise definition, and their failure—even greater than that of most cultures—to prescribe with any clarity the scope of the terms they use, the Japanese also applied the term Shintō to, or subsumed under the broad wing of the words 'Shintō ceremony', a host of folk and traditional practices many of which, not unnaturally in localities where the Shintō shrine was the main or even the only focus of community life, became attached to or were celebrated at such a shrine. The parade of twenty tall floats through the main streets of Kyōto on July 17th is under the patronage of the Gion Shrine, for it was the head priest there who, over a thousand years ago, led the first procession in an attempt to rid the capital of a raging epidemic. Gion Festival is now little other than a traditional holiday parade. Yet, participation in this parade, classified as a Shintō ritual in that it is celebrated from a Shintō Shrine, was condemned as nationalistic and reactionary and was banned for several years at the end of the war, much to the bewilderment of Gion's parishioners. For, when they took part in their great festival of the year, they believed not that they were lending themselves to some warlike activity but that they did merely 'what comes naturally'. Many of the 'spirits' of the 'Way of the Spirits' are those of ancestors. So Shintō is often a synonym for 'doing as our forefathers did'; so 'acting in true Japanese fashion', so 'acting naturally'. Hence the definition of Shintō by an accomplished expert in both Shintō and Buddhism (Jiun, in the eighteenth century), as 'this pure Japanese naturalness, this spontaneity'.

In the years before contact with Buddhism and for a long period after the foreign faith had begun to influence it, Shintō lacked all trace of a moral imperative. Ceremonial purity and the absence of ritual pollution were the only prerequisites for and often the entire goal of worship and service. Provided the hands were clean, the body outwardly unsmudged, it mattered not how filthy the mind or the heart beneath. For it was the technical correctness of the approach made to them, the formal precision and beauty of diction of the *norito* (songs of praise) intoned for their hearing that attracted the spirits and compelled their attention and care. Hence the words of the Sun Goddess when, according to the myth, locked in the Rock Cave of Heaven she heard the ode of praise performed beyond the doorway to cajole her from her retreat—'It is long indeed since I have heard a prayer whose beauty of language was so striking as this.' Hence, also, Shintō's ability to ignore the fact of the good heart or the conscience, even after a long period of contact with Buddhism. It is only in the early fourteenth century that Shintō arrives at a clear distinction between physical and moral rectitude; thus—'If one washes himself in sea water and is cleansed of bodily filth, this is outer purity. But if we are pure in mind and body, our soul is united with the divine, and divinity in humanity is thus realized.'

The insistence on physical purity as a prerequisite of participation in worship or ritual, and the attainment of non-pollution in the course of or as a result of the performance of a ceremony is still today the essential purpose of the greater part of the ceremonies we shall discuss. Blood, the 'red' pollution, the most tainting form of uncleanliness, was, according to a ninth century text, a tabooed word on no account to be mentioned in the same breath with the sacred shrine of the Sun Goddess at Ise: *ase*—perspiration—was to be employed in its stead. Until not many years ago, women in childbirth and even during menstrual periods were segregated and relegated to live in dark and cheerless hovels until, cleared of pollution after a stipulated term, they might return to the contacts and duties of everyday life: there are even hints that the consummation of marriage, entailing the letting of blood and consequent 'red' pollution, was similarly at one stage confined to special houses set apart from the normal residential area of the community. Salt, the sophistication of ritual sea bathing as a cleanser of contamination, appears today even in many apparently secular uses. The *sumō* wrestler will sprinkle it across the ring as he advances from his corner to take up his crouching stance ready for the grapple; he does this merely to ensure external formality and rectitude—this is no symbolic act springing from a mind imbued with an Olympic love of fair play. A pinch of salt is often put by the side of a well and a restaurant frequently has its Fuji-cone of caked salt by the door-jamb, as a means of clearing the defilement left by an unwelcome patron. As often as not, the man who has spent the night in a red-light bed will sprinkle his body and his clothes with salt before his return home. And—one of the quaintest demonstrations of this fetish for the absence of filth—even the mud at the roots of the rice shoots bedded out in the riceplanting ritual is washed and cleansed.

Who, then, are the spirits of Shintō, the *kami* who make such stringent demands for and have so delicate an appreciation of ritual purity and perfection? The word *kami* is something of a free-for-all for the Japanese etymologist. The most common explanation relates it to a homonym meaning 'upper' or 'the head': the *kami* are thus superior or head beings who reside on a plane spatially higher than the human. Or *kami* is interpreted as related to a word meaning 'to see', with a cognate in *kagami*, a mirror. Thus it could be said, in the fourteenth century, 'The *kami*, like a mirror, reflects all things in nature; it allows not one taint of uncleanness.' Another analysis derives the word from a fusion of *kaburi* and *mi*, a hidden body or person, and along similar lines it is explained as meaning 'face of hidden mystery'.

Faulty in method though these latter interpretations might be, they yet lead to the happiest and most likely solution, for, in the words of the great eighteenth century Shintō thinker Motoori, *kami* is 'anything at all beyond the ordinary, or with superior power, or anything awe-inspiring. Thus there are *kami* of many kinds—some are noble, some are base, some are good, some bad.' Thus, although the spirits of the dead comprise the bulk of the *kami* host, it is not by any means only they who are possessed of *kami* potentiality. The sea or the mountains have it in virtue of their awesome nature, as does, for example, a dwarf, an albino, an exceptionally large or abnormally shaped tree or stone.

It is not very far from Japan's *kami* to Polynesia's *mana*. Once more, in the similarity in Japan and Polynesia of the concept itself and of much of the ritual which revolves round the person or the object possessing this quality, there is evidence of at least a partial connection between the Japanese stock and the Southern Pacific. By *mana* the Pacific islander connotes a force beyond the ordinary but yet distinct from sheer physical power. The *mana*-body is awesome and potentially dangerous, so it is best avoided; if it must needs be approached then ritual preparations ensuring freedom from pollution are the safest prophylactics before contact is essayed.

This is exactly the signification of Motoori's definition of *kami* as 'beyond the ordinary, possessing superior power or awe-inspiring': in Japan as in the Pacific cultures, all contact with entities having *kami* potentiality should be safeguarded by ceremonial designed to effect the absence of impurity. There is little doubt both from records of the early myths and from many ritual practices still observed that these *kami* were imagined as living in their own world—in all respects a replica of Japan—on a plane physically higher than the latter. In the creation story, Izanagi and Izanami, the *kami* creator couple, dangled a long spear from their world on high until its tip was submerged in the sea. The brine drips from their spear coagulated and solidified to form the islands of Japan; we shall revert later to this conception of the great purifying agent—salt in this instance—as the basic material of all creation. The use of high banners or standards in a number of festivals today also indicates that the *kami* whose presence the celebration induces and honours is thought of as descending from above to the site of the ceremony, for these tall poles and pillars are intended as runway markers in much the same way as the Christmas Tree serves, in part, as an aid to Santa Claus's navigational accuracy.

However, when development brought the construction of permanent shrine buildings, many of the *kami* found a home on this earthly plane. But there were and are still not a few who commute to the site of a ceremony from a distant residence or from an alternative home. Customary Japanese vagueness, intensified in this sort of context, precludes firm conclusions about the location of the starting terminus of such *kami* journeys but at least it is certain that one class of *kami*, of the paddy and of the mountains, is conceived of as commuting at fixed times in the year between its two protectorates.

By far the greater part of the entities to which *kami* potential is attributed are beneficent, for the general stamp of Japanese religious observance has always been that of love and gratitude rather than of fear and terror. The purpose of ritual generally is not to propitiate so much as to thank and praise and so to please and vouchsafe perpetuation of the accustomed benignity. Malevolence on the part of the *kami* is as a rule a mark of such spirits as were at one time harmful in life or who have been consigned to a destitute and joyless existence in the *kami* world through either the loss of all connection with their descendants or the lack of any such to perform ceremonies in their honour.

If they are benign and work good for you it is right, especially in a land where the most meticulous attention is given to the ritual exchange of gifts, that you desire to have the *kami* among you to receive your thanks and to watch— even to take part in—your celebrations in honour of the harvest and other blessings that their goodwill has ensured. But to be qualified to welcome so splendid a visitor, you must be free from any contamination, for the very first thing he will notice on arrival is the outward cleanliness of your person and the precision and perfection of your approach to him. Hence, as a prelude to any important celebration at which the attendance of the *kami* is anticipated, there is often a stipulated period of *komori*, a ritual fasting and abstention. *Komori* often takes the form of a vigil, a voluntary incarceration, held either in the village shrine or often in some community building. It was the main feature of the rainmaking ritual in one village (see Chapter Six); members of each of the sixty-four households in the village, taking on the duty by rotation, kept a week's vigil by the side of a holy flame in the local Agricultural Advisory Hall. So vital is it in Japanese eyes to remove all trace of pollution that there are even instances where preparatory purification and subsequent festival merge into one. In one celebration—if it can be called such—in Shimane Prefecture, for the whole of the six days of the ritual, music, needlework, building construction, the cutting of hair and clipping of nails, and the refurbishing of the paper panes of the wooden partition doors of the Japanese house are all taboo.

But the essential purpose of the *komori* is preparatory and purificatory. Originally, the whole of a geographical or social grouping touched by the *kami*'s actions—in the case of a territorial *kami* every inhabitant of the soil under his tutelage —was expected to join in the observance of the *komori* for

26

a period even as long as a month. Now, a week at the most, more often two or three days, are considered sufficient, and it is a measure of the power and social preponderance of family over individual that, provided that a single representative of each household attends, that household is regarded as having fully discharged its obligations. The headman of the rainmaking village numbered his charges by households; it was in such terms that he answered the question 'What is the population of your village?' When pressed to give the number of heads, he had to ponder for some time and then replied in round figures, prefixing the number with the 'about' so dear to the Japanese.

Komori, then, is essentially a community function, to be attended by every member, or, less strictly, his representative, of the association concerned in the ceremony which it precedes. Such community-mindedness, the insistence on all taking their share, is another recurrent feature of Japanese ceremonial observance. It stems in part from a strong streak of perfectionism in the Japanese character: it is also a matter of simple courtesy, where the *kami*-guest is so distinguished, that each one of his intending hosts be ritually clean and fitted to welcome him. Further, since at any crucial juncture, such as the dividing point of the seasons, freedom from contamination serves as a safeguard, it is vital that there be not a single defaulter to prove the fatal niche in the armour of community purification. Hence, in the many joint undertakings of Japanese life (which are diminishing rapidly in number and scope—the west's legacy of self-sufficiency has been put to extended use) default has always been treated as a pernicious offence, not to be permitted to go unpunished. Sanctions are easily applied, for any house that bilks its obligations can be refused the use of jointly-owned agricultural tools or aids; it might find the water supply cut off from its paddy, it may be denied the benefits of the new experimental arc-lights designed to lure blight-pests away from the ripening rice, and it is not difficult to withdraw the community assistance readily given in rural areas to any family stricken by the calamity of death, typhoon or flood ravage, and so on. If such economic methods fail to have effect, there yet remains the far more cogent sanction of ridicule. In any situation in Japan, fear of being laughed at is one of the most powerful spurs to conformity and acquiescence, *haji* (the sense of shame for action that may provoke ridicule) a most effective and universal deterrent.

Having abstained for a while from their normal activities and functions through the *komori*, those who are to celebrate a festival are ready to welcome the *kami* to their midst. The Japanese word usually translated as festival is *matsuri*, the nominal form of a verb meaning 'to work' or 'to do a service at the side of a personage of high status'. This performance of service, at the banquet when the worshippers, in company with the *kami*, partake of the offerings they have made him, is the core of and the clue to the significance of the various activities contained within the *matsuri*. Around this banquet cluster all the courtesies with which the distinguished guest would be treated. At most *matsuri* and especially at the two great ceremonies dividing the year, New Year and Bon, elaborate preparations are made at the spot to which the *kami* are thought to return (or where they have their permanent or semi-permanent residence), along the route thence to the site of the *matsuri*, and at the site itself, the household in the case of an ancestral festival. Decorations adorn some if not all these points, bonfires often mark the expected point of arrival of the *kami* and winking torches guide their steps to their home during the *matsuri*. At the annual festival of the tutelary *kami* of a shrine near Kyōto, for a week before celebrations proper begin, the roof of every house belonging to parishioners of the shrine is distinguished by a branch of the *sakaki*, Japan's sacred evergreen. The purpose of this adornment is twofold for, first, the *sakaki* is purificatory and so fulfils a role similar to that of the *komori*; again, if each roof of the community bears a *sakaki* branch, the approaching *kami* may more easily discern his parish and is no doubt gladdened that every member of it intends to take part in his festival. An elaboration of this practice occurs in another village not far from the first, where, as well as every

28

house, the village boundaries also bear the distinguishing and cleansing *sakaki* branch.

Then comes the community banquet, often called *naorai*, a 'face to face encounter', when *kami* and parishioner share the joint food of man's offerings, offerings brought to maturity by the *kami's* beneficence.

In the final part of the ritual of the *matsuri*, the *kami*, amply provided for his journey, is escorted with all respect either beyond the community confines or to the site considered most appropriate for his departure. The spirit boat, a feature common to most Pacific territories, appears also in Japan, for example at the end of the Bon festival, as the means of conveying the ancestors (or *kami*) safely back to their home, home, in this instance, being generally regarded as far over the seas.

If a penchant for purity is one constant feature running through the whole of Shintō ceremonial and the folk practices of the Japanese, their fondness for growth and detestation of any form of decay is another. The latter appears distinctly enough in the creation myth. On her death after giving birth to the deity of fire, the female of the divine creator couple descended to the 'Land of Darkness'. There, she was visited by the male creator: the aspect of this world of decay revolted him, for 'putrefying matter had gushed up within her, and maggots swarmed like unto the flies of the fifth moon'. (Japan's June flies, clinging and obese, swarm eagerly around any form of flesh.)

Although, like the other crises of the life cycle, death involves contamination (the 'black' pollution) it is the one with which Shintō ritual has throughout been least concerned. The contamination of the 'red' pollution may be the more dangerous and widespread, yet, once the crisis is over and the concomitant defilement purged, life and growth ensue. The 'black' pollution is the herald of the onset of decay and decomposition which can be viewed only with distaste.

This Japanese predilection for growth, the stress put on the greenness of life, may be the explanation of the wide ceremonial use of the *sakaki*, for one derivation of the word breaks it down into *sakae* and *ki*, the 'flourishing tree'. If this derivation be correct, it would be by no means an isolated instance of the practice of sympathetic magic by the use of a play on words. *Kiku*, the chrysanthemum, used in certain autumn *matsuri* is homonymous with a word meaning 'to be efficacious'; *daidai*, the large bitter orange adorning many new year decorations, may also signify 'for generation upon generation'; and in our rainmaking village we shall come upon the drought-stricken farmers trying to effect the fall of rain (*furu*) by brandishing (*furu*) a sacred flame for the entire length of its thirty-odd mile journey to the spot where it was to be the centre of the vigil. Certainly, at the root of the general use of pine, bamboo and other evergreens at a great many *matsuri*—the most important of which are to mark and to tide the celebrants over the critical juncture of a change of season—must be the thought that the year-round vitality of such trees can be transferred magically to aid both season and farmer. This notion is very apparent in the following wedding banquet song.

> Rejoice. Be happy.
> The young pine's
> Branches flourish;
> Its leaves grow thick.
> The house, too, thrives,
> Children increase.[1]

But perhaps the most striking instance of this fondness for perfection and vitality is the belief, still commonly held in many fishing or seashore communities, that birth comes with the rising or the full tide, death with the ebb. The child born when the tide is on the ebb will be a weakling or will die young; that born with the tide rising or at the full will live long and strong.

There is little doubt that the Japanese love of completeness and fullness is not unconnected with the siting of most of the important year-round *matsuri* on the night of the full

[1] See J. F. Embree, *Japanese Peasant Songs*, Philadelphia, 1944.

moon. Only a very small part of ceremonial practice falls during the dark of the moon and the rituals celebrated on or near the night of the first quarter, while in general less important than those of the full moon, are still of greater moment than those of the last quarter. The lyrics of one harvest moon song urge all and sundry to indulge in sexual relations this night; continence invites the devils' pestle-pounding in the next life.

Japan used the lunar calendar for official purposes until the second half of the last century and it is still, in fact, the only dating system recognized by the greater part of farming and fishing activities. Hence the close adherence of the *matsuri* calendar to the moon's course, for festive celebration and rice production are intimately interwoven. Like most civilizations, the early Japanese adopted the lunar cycle as the basis for the division of the year into months and at first it was the time of the full moon that was reckoned as the start of the month. This honour accorded to the moon by Japan's first calendar compilers may appear inconsistent with the primacy that those who narrated her creation myths gave to the sun. According to the latter, it was from the cleansing of his defilement contracted in the 'Land of Darkness' at the time of his visit to the putrefying first female that the first male created sun and moon. The former, the elder sister, sprang from the washing of his left eye, the latter, the younger brother, from the right eye—no trace here of ideas of dexterity, none of the sinister associations of the left (though I have yet to see a Japanese who wrote with his left hand)! To the primitive farmer, however (and fisherman, through the connection between moon and tide) the moon's course is a deal more constant than the sun's and thus affords a more sure basis for calculation. The woman, too, can reckon by the moon and anticipate the onset of her menstrual flow, an aspect of 'red' pollution, the most heinous of all impurities. And though the sun may bring untold benefits to the farmer, the sight of the full moon is the more impressive and inspiring; Japan's poets and writers throughout her history have been just as moonstruck as the west's pop song

lyricists of the past twenty years. Thus, an eleventh century
lady of the court made the following entry in her diary:

'Men have always disputed the charms of the seasons. The
haze that veils the spring has its own appeal for then the sky is
tranquil and the visage of the moon is not over-bright;
dimmed by the mist, its rays shine dreamily as on a river
rippling far away. If at such a moment you hear the gentle
plucking of the lute, its notes are exquisitely enchanting.
But, on an autumn night, with cloud wisps trailing through
the sky, the moon yet seems so close and limpid that you
could reach out your hand and grasp it. On such a night,
when the rustle of the warm breeze melts with the chirping
of the insects and creates a unity that sinks into your heart,
if you hear the sounds of harp or flute, you dismiss the
claims of spring and resolve that all the fascinations of the
seasons belong to autumn.

'Then again, there is the sky of a midwinter night glister-
ing in the crisp air. If, when the moon's rays sparkle on the
water pearls of the bedded snowdrift, you hear the plaintive
tune of the reed-pipe pierce the dead-still night, then
autumn and spring are forgotten on the instant.'

(Sarashina Nikki)

But though the full moon was the most impressive to
primitive minds (especially to those susceptible to fullness
and perfection), the art of writing which enables the handling
of a written calendar brings with it a swing of importance to
the beginning of the moon's course, the period of the dark
of the moon and the new moon, hitherto insignificant and
almost bereft of year-round ceremonials. So calendrical
practice also suffered considerable change as a result of the
wholesale adoption of Chinese-dominated continental culture. Among such new elements was the double or redupli-
cated number so dear to the Chinese mind, such as the first
day of the first month, the third of the third month and so
on. The number selected for such reduplication was usually
odd, where indigenous preference had been overwhelmingly

32

for the even. Not a single odd number—and none of them are couched in round terms—occurs in records in early Chinese dynastic histories listing the gifts brought to the Chinese court by Japanese embassies from the third century AD onwards. Japan's magic and mystic number is the even eight; eight-forked serpents slither through the episodes of the creation myths, eight-bladed swords flash as they wield themselves, Japan is a domain of eight thousand islands and, even today, the greengrocer is, literally, the 'eight hundred item shopman'.

Yet, in spite of the incorporation of such new elements and of memorial and commemorative celebrations derived from Buddhist and Confucian history, the indigenous system was never deluged or jettisoned. As a result, Japan's *matsuri* calendar soon took on the cosmopolitan hue which it retains to this day. Go into a farming village a mere five miles from the centre of Kyōto and you will find, at best, only token recognition given to the official festival calendar celebrated in urban centres by bank holidays, flag-flying from public buildings and the like. January 1st, April 29th, the present Emperor's Birthday, November 3rd (the birthday of Emperor Meiji which, since the Occupation tried its hand at refurbishing this heterogeneous system and added a state-side veneer, has become Culture Day) often pass more or less unmarked in the countryside. Where almost everyone concerned with the calendar derives this concern from his engagement in production from the land or the sea, the ritual year and the inception of almost every major agricultural task are still guided by the course of the moon.

The picture becomes even more confused when it is realized that practically every farmer and fisherman still reckons the start of the year from the old lunar first month, coinciding roughly with the early part of the second month of the official solar system. However, the reason for rural conservatism in this matter is soon apparent. To the farmer, what can be the point in signalling the start of the new year and the end of winter, the stir of new life in his soil, at a time when snow lies on the ground, when every plant and

tree is blackened by the frost and there is no visible indication of the rebirth he is meant to be welcoming and abetting
by his celebrations? Yet by the old lunar calculation, the
start of the farmer's new year coincides appropriately with
the first signs of reawakening life as the plum tree blossoms.
There is then a deal of point in repairing your year-round
tools, escorting your *kami* into your village, feasting with him
and sending him off content that your household is well
ordered and deserving of aid through the hard months to
come.

The rural *matsuri* calendar is naturally regulated in intimate
co-ordination with the year's work of the farmer. This is
bound up with the rice crop, his primary and most time-
consuming occupation: any other activity, a harvest of millet
or oats, even a tobacco crop, likely to be much more of a
money spinner, is counted of far less importance and is
merely fitted in when and where the rice allows. So most of
the rural *matsuri* that have grown out of the year-round tasks
of the rice crop find no counterpart in the culture of other
staple crops. Hence, in the year's festival calendar, while
such rituals as are directly concerned with rice—planting
and the rest—either precede or follow on immediately
after the appropriate activity in the rice year, others not so
related fall at intervals of a break between labours when the
farmer is free for a while to lift his thoughts out of the ruts in
his paddy. The fourth and fifth months of the lunar calendar
(May and June in official reckoning) are among the busiest
of the entire year; rice transplanting is often preceded by the
wheat harvest and, in some areas, the spring tasks of seri-
culture must be found a place. Throughout this intensely
busy period many rural areas celebrate hardly a single
matsuri of any moment; then, in the middle of the fifth
month, with transplanting finished, there follows a holiday
often lasting several days and involving considerable *matsuri*
activity. It is in a situation of this nature that the Japanese
displays his ingenuity in handling his various imports and
turning to his own ends their often conflicting claims. The
Boys' Festival, celebrated on one of the Chinese-style

'double' days, the fifth of the fifth month, is frequently observed in the countryside according to the official calendar on May 5th, before this period of heavy work reaches its height, where, by the lunar calendar, festival and labour peak coincide.

Conversely, *matsuri* come thick and fast during the slack periods in the farmer's year. To add to traditionally rural celebrations, the farmer has adapted festivals essentially urban in origin. He reshaped them to a format more akin to that of the *matsuri* of his clan or community *kami* and transferred them from their original celebration date either to one more suited to the slack seasons of the rice year or to such as blend with the lunar pattern of the other local rites.

The original purpose of the majority of *matsuri* was to meet the guardian *kami* and to guarantee his continued protection and customary benevolence: the face-to-face meeting— *naorai*—was essentially a quiet and dignified ceremony in the presence of an august guest. Then, as the basic significance of the year-round *matsuri* began gradually to fade, the festival day came to be regarded rather as a time of rest from labour and an excuse for, or even an inducement to, license and riotous celebration. The change from courteous and digni- fied calm to boisterous and frenzied caperings was assisted by the gradual spread to almost every corner of Japan of the noisier and more spirited ceremonies concerned with the exorcism of plague deities or 'hungry' and so angered spirits. Although of the sixty thousand registered Shintō shrines in Japan more than ninety-nine per cent began as centres of the more dignified type of *matsuri*, based on the *komori* and *naorai* of *kami* and parishioner, this latter style of ceremony of necessity paled by comparison with the noisy and spectacular procession of the *mikoshi* (the portable ark for the *kami*) or the *yamaboko* (the tall float) which is the central part of the Gion Festival, the most famous of a group designed originally to drive out the spirit of the plague. As could only be expected, as the latter spread from its home site to become a nation-wide ritual, it enlivened the quiet formality of the former. Again it is only natural that the more spectacular has captured the interest of the indigenous as well as the foreign observer.

In the chapters that follow I shall attempt to describe and explain both of these basic *matsuri* forms. The rainmaking ritual, for example, is intrinsically the community ceremony paying due regard to the various elements of the local *kami* type of festival—*komori*, joint feasting, promises of offerings and the like. New Year and Bon celebrations also, in spite of much local variation and eccentricity, are essentially the entertainment at two fixed points in the year of ancestral and local spirits, designed to secure the continuation of their goodwill, on the one hand at the start of spring with all its preparatory tasks culminating in the rice planting and, on the other, at the threshold of autumn and the harvest. Gion Matsuri, however, traditionally originates from a ceremony designed to stay the course of an epidemic raging through Kyōto in the latter part of the ninth century and is the prototype for a number of parallel spectacles worthy of all the adjectives of the film trailer.

The study of folk practices is comparatively young in Japan. But both the amateur enthusiast and the bookworming scholar have much on their side. For ample repayment may come from a week's stay in a mountain village in a backwater more or less unruffled by the eddies of all the earlier as well as the more recent flood waters of modernization, westernization, sinification, and the rest—though the surface scum may bear readily discernible traces of these various deluges. Patient reading of the literary evidence such as the village diary (compiled by the headman at a New Year community gathering and noting all the important events of the year just passed—something like the New Year newsreels or the BBC Scrapbook) can be just as fruitful. And here, once more, the museum-type mentality of the Japanese, their urge at all costs to preserve and refurbish, is a godsend.

It is in this sort of context, too, that one may find some constituents of the long-needed antidote to the hasty sketches of Japan's urban scene by the short-term foreign observer who portrays almost every Japanese as the potential if not actual schizophrenic, as ideal suicide material. Everywhere in Japan there is abuse of the foreign import—primarily that from the west though very occasionally that from the neighbouring civilizations of the east—the radio, the commercial TV (a still in the course of a Kabuki drama; a facial posture by one of the stars, teeth bared, and the caption 'Yes! I Lion'd my teeth this morning'), the car horn, the *kamikaze* taxi and so on, as well as the distortions in the long list of ideas adopted. But go to the mountain village and, if you can dispense with the incomprehending student or *Nisei* interpreter, such abuse becomes much less significant in face of the perfect appropriateness and delicate susceptibility of the use of the indigenous. (The city, too, has this delicacy in no small measure, but it is often suffocated and overwhelmed by the other.) Of course the Arbeit Salon or the Jazz and Tea Parlour are fair game for banter and a host of jibes: but you swallow these back hastily when you talk to the seventy year old farmer about his village Bon dance, and he tells you stories he has known since childhood, in surroundings to which he has been perfectly integrated for as long as he could move his legs or his mind. Now, all the stumbling hesitations, all the mixed-up craziness of the amphibious townee are gone; and, with them, go a deal of the question marks and the tasteless taunts of the foreigner.

Japan's folk practices are often keys to her way of life, to the thought processes and the modes of belief of her people: their study gives generous repayment not only to the foreigner but—as Dr Yanagida, Japan's foremost folklorist, insisted so often—to many a Japanese himself.

Two

THE NEW YEAR

The Japanese will adopt and adapt just about anything. One late nineteenth century observer mentions earnest top-level discussions going on in his day on the suitability of April Fool's Day for incorporation into the Japanese year-round festival calendar; the decision finally went against the proposal—a rare instance of discrimination—but whatever official circles decreed, there must have been a certain

New Year door decorations

degree of private initiative, for nowadays mention of the phrase '*shigatsu baka*', fourth-month fool, draws more than a blank stare of incomprehension from many a face, and there are not a few households—some of them with a fine regard for tradition—where blocks of wood replace rice balls or sandwiches in lunch tins, or where salt goes into the coffee on April 1st.

But the eager curiosity to taste the new never quite masters the age-old attention for and appreciation of the old. So the two, the old home-bred custom and the new, often foreign, practice are maintained side by side, frequently quite distinct, the one hardly influencing the other. This is especially evident in the matter of the festival calendar. The year-round observances of the farming and fishing village bear only an occasional resemblance to the official almanac, while city and town ceremonies are at best vaguely reflected in the country-side. Among Japan's various yearly rituals, the coexistence of the old alongside the new is reflected perhaps most distinctly in the complicated aspect of the numerous cere-monies that go to make up the New Year festival.

By the traditional calendar, regulated by the moon, New Year and Bon, the All Souls' Feast, divided the year; both were centred on the fifteenth day—that of the full moon—the one of the first month, the other of the seventh. Both were essentially identical in character, being soul festivals, their purpose to welcome home the spirits of family an-cestors, share a joint feast with them, divine their wills at the critical juncture of the seasons for the period to come, and then to send them off with fires to light their going. That this joining of the seasons was uppermost in men's minds during the New Year festival is clear from the frequency with which the word *setsu* (or *setchi*) occurs in application to different elements of the celebrations. *Setsu* means, origin-ally, the knot or joint in a stem of bamboo; used of the year, it refers to the joints of the year—the meeting points of the seasons, or of the larger half-year divisions. So, the firewood prepared by children for the vigil on New Year's Eve is often given the name *setchigi*—the 'wood of the year's joining'; the title 'dividing day' is accorded to the second day of the New Year in fishing communities in the western part of the main island, and in the area about Kyōto the food eaten on New Year's Eve is often known by the name 'Year's Knot'.

However, the change of stress from the centre to the beginning of the month and the introduction of the solar calendar both helped to blur the basic identity of New Year and Bon, for while the ritual of the latter remained with its focus on the full moon of the middle of the month, many of the New Year ceremonies were switched to the early part of the first or the last days of the twelfth month. But there was no uniformity about this process, with the result that a ceremony that may be observed in one part of the country on its old day, the fifteenth of the first month, has been transferred to the beginning of the month elsewhere. Nowadays, it almost seems that there are two parallel New Year festivals, celebrated two weeks apart from each other; but two broad divisions of practice can be distinguished. The first is that while the Tōhoku area, in the north-east part of the main island, has preserved and tends to give more attention to the celebrations centred on the middle of the month (called 'Little New Year'), the western part of the mainland gives more stress to New Year proper. Again, the urban centres follow the official calendar more readily while to the people of the farming and fishing villages who still regulate their work timetable by the moon and the tides, the 'Little New Year' of the old lunar system is clearly the more beneficial and appropriate.

This deep divergence of practice makes it difficult to construct anything in the way of a standard timetable for the numerous New Year activities. The urban New Year festival can be dismissed fairly summarily as comprising a series of practices preparatory for and leading up to the New Year—the clearing of debts, the preparation of food, and especially the pounding of *mochi* (rice-cakes) ready for the day—then, on New Year's Day itself and the first few days of the month (official holidays), formal visits to relatives, branch house to main house and so on, to friends, and to business or craft associates. This is perhaps an over-simplification of the urban celebration of the festival, for many houses still observe a number of the practices we shall describe in their rural context, but the latter deserves more attention in that it is intrinsically of greater interest and provides a truer indication of both the original aspect and the underlying purpose of the ceremony as a whole. In the country as well, however, practice is by no means standard: in some areas, the calendar reform has been accepted and incorporated, with the result that New Year's Day has usurped the position of the fifteenth of the first month as the central point of the series of celebrations; in others the latter staunchly retains its old importance, while in yet further examples, the Japanese art of incorporation—and compromise where incorporation involves incongruence—has led to the observance of parallel ceremonies on each occasion.

At New Year many distinctive foods are prepared and eaten, their names frequently involving a magic play on meanings. On the thirteenth of the twelfth month a special stew is prepared from red beans, sliced fish, and *konnyaku*, a root the length of which may make it a long life charm—certainly it has phallic connotations in folk-songs from several different areas of Japan. Also properly performed on the thirteenth day of the last month is a series of ceremonies given the name 'New Year Rising'; such ceremonies include the gathering of the firewood that is to be used for the first fire of the New Year, a general house-cleaning (part practical, part ritual) which extends to the sweeping of soot from all places where it may have gathered and the changing of the fire in the hearth. *Mochi* for the New Year was traditionally pounded on this day which was also the occasion for formal visits and greetings from the inferior to his superior—branch to main house, apprentice to craftsman, and so on.

There can be little doubt that the occurrence on a date as early as December 13th of this variety of ceremonies—most of them of considerable importance and properly, it would seem, performed immediately prior to the New Year—results from a trick of the dual calendar. Originally a purificatory prelude to the lunar New Year, when the day of the full moon was reckoned as the start of the month, they were performed two days before the 'Little New Year'—the fifteenth of the first month. Then, with the development of the concept of the new moon as the month beginning, and with the change to the solar calendar, instead of retaining their original day as a natural prelude to the 'Little New Year' which kept many of its observances, these preparations were switched to the only date possible, the thirteenth of the twelfth month if, as evidently happened, they were not to lose their intimate connection with the thirteenth day.

Some of the *mochi* that is pounded on the thirteenth is used to make the 'mirror *mochi*', two circular cakes, the smaller resting on the larger, that is always evident in New Year decorations. The 'mirror *mochi*' may well derive from the first use, in Japanese myth, of the mirror to entice the Sun Goddess out of her Rock Cave of Heaven after her disappearance had plunged the world into darkness; when thoughts turn to the crops of the New Year, the weakened power of the sun must be drawn out and assisted at this critical juncture of the seasons. It is decked with four leaves of the laurel which point to the four directions—for the old laurel leaves still cling firmly to the branch after the young ones have appeared, and thus symbolize the united family and all its branches wherever dispersed; it is also garnished with ears of corn, dried persimmons, sardines and roasted chestnuts; the word for the latter is reminiscent in sound of that for 'victory'—presumably over all the farmers' tasks of the year to come.

The doorway decorations almost always include the straw rope (an indication of taboo in the greater part of the Pacific area and again, in the myth of the Rock Cave, used to delimit the boundary which the Sun Goddess was not to cross once she had been lured from her hiding place) which is made with the strands twisted towards the left, the pure or fortunate side—the exact antithesis of Roman notions of the location of the sinister and the dexterous. A variety of objects may festoon this rope: there is the large bitter orange the name of which, *daidai*, may also signify 'generation upon generation', the lobster, its bent back symbolizing long life, and white-backed fern fronds which spring in pairs from the stem and stand for a happy and fruitful married union. But the most important part of the New Year decorations is the 'door pine'—a misnomer since bamboo and plum often stand alongside the pine branch. At the left of the door stands the 'red pine', a variety with a red wood trunk, at the right a black wood trunk species; the red of the left symbolizes the female—as the Sun Goddess was created from the cleansing of the left eye—and the black stands for the male. But the 'door pine' is more than simple decoration: it is regarded as the temporary home, or even the concrete 'spirit body' of the *kami* who returns for the New Year festival. So the ceremony of 'welcoming the pine' is more than a simple visit to the hills to select a suitably sized branch; it is the ritual of escorting the returning spirits from their place of abode— the *kami* of the paddy spends his slack season in the mountains—or from their touch down point after a journey from the woolly far distance where ancestral spirits are imagined to reside. And in the same way, the New Year fires, fed by the various forms of decoration, constitute the ritual of sending off such *kami* at the time of their return.

Sometimes, the 'year tree' forms another principal piece of the New Year decorations. Usually, the 'year tree' is a branch set up in the centre of the house (the spot regarded as sacred to Daikoku, the god of wealth) but it may also be a bale of straw. Originally this 'year tree' was the basic fuel of the two early New Year fire festivals—that to drive away evil spirits on the seventh day (for which there is an exact parallel in the Tanabata Festival, celebrated on the seventh day of the seventh month, and clearly, in part a purification ritual in preparation for Bon on the fifteenth) and that of 'Little New Year' on the fifteenth. If the ashes of the 'year tree', after burning, are strewn around the compound, they will drive off all poisonous insects, if put under the eaves, they will protect the house from lightning and the thunderbolt, and in some districts, this ash is saved and used to cook the rice used in ceremonies connected with rice transplanting, almost at the close of the period of the year during which these practices guarantee protection and good fortune.

Water, in that it is one of the main purifying agents, must be kept free of pollution or renewed in some way at all moments of crisis. So, before the sun's rays on the first day

'*Young Water*' *is drawn before sunrise on New Year's Day*

of the year fall on it, 'young' water is drawn and is used either for the infusion of the 'lucky' tea of the New Year, or to cook the first meal and thus ensure good health. In many areas, the 'young' water custom has lapsed; once it was one of the most important tasks of the 'year male', the male member of the household chosen, or bound by his position of seniority, to fill the role of making all preparations, selecting and escorting the door pine, seeing to offerings and so on. Such duties, in some districts, were once viewed as being of sufficient moment to warrant the 'year male' sleeping immediately before the shelf of the *kami* (where the offerings were set out) and lying on a couch of straw matting on each of the first seven nights of the New Year. Elsewhere, and especially in western Japan, 'young' water was often drawn by the senior woman in a household, who would offer *mochi*, sometimes called 'water mirror', at the well.

The name given to food eaten on the final day of the old year indicates the nature of the whole series of ceremonies. Sometimes it is called *toshitori*, 'taking a year', and if you eat long *soba* noodles, the number of years you add will be increased; otherwise, and more frequently in the western half of Japan, this food may be called 'the meal of the year joint'; thoughts turn to and hopes are high for an auspicious beginning of the coming portion of the year, for, technically, the next day is the first day of spring. Though the reforms make a nonsense of it all, according to the old dating the plum tree would be in blossom and would herald the return of life to the soil and to the sea. So a good many New Year practices, and especially those of 'Little New Year', point towards the countless tasks in the field that will absorb energies in the months to come. 'Mirror-*mochi*' is often offered to a sack of unhulled rice; *mochi* is regarded as one of the most precious offerings, and it is fitting that rice in the raw, representing the crop that is to be tended through the greater part of the coming year, should be the recipient at this juncture. The other ceremony often practised on the eve of the New Year is the 'year vigil'; the vigil, *komori*, the means of attaining ceremonial purity, renders its celebrant fit to meet the year deity or the returning ancestral spirits.

No doubt all of the above observances have slipped back from their proper position as ceremonies preparatory to the main festival of 'Little New Year'. Certainly, in most instances, there is now a long blank in most calendars until the period immediately prior to the mid-month festival. The eleventh is often the day chosen for the year's first performance of an action or task that is due to be repeated a good many times in the year to come. Where hill forests are worked by a village, the men make their first ceremonial climb up to the lumber sites and 'welcome the young wood'. In some instances, it is believed that the year spirit returns with them to the village. The 'year-*kami*' has many affinities with the *kami* of the paddy, who spends the close season in the hills, and is thought to return to the paddy ready for transplanting; both are offered unpolished rice and both are commonly thought to depart from their temporary festival home on the 'day of the hare'—of the first month in the case of the year-*kami* and of the fifth (lunar) month for the *kami* of the paddy. Similarly, work will be started on one of the countless uses to which straw is put. As will be amply evident from later examples, straw is a powerful purifier as well as an extremely useful all-purpose commodity, so that it is especially appropriate that it be worked at a time when the seasons merge. The fisherman makes his first boat trip of the year, the woman diver enters the sea, and, on the same day in some areas, firewood is collected and then stored away ready for heating the rice which will be used for the offerings and for the feast of the transplanting festival. In the northeast there used to be a fairly widespread practice whereby the male members of a house each made small bundles of straw and offered them with New Year decorations, such as pine branches, *mochi* and *sake* to a tree growing within the household compound; branches of this tree were then cut and made into a fire and the offertory *sake*, heated over this fire, was then drunk. Perhaps the year-*kami* or the household ancestral spirits used this tree as their marker or their

46

resting place during their stay; in either case their contact with it would impart to it great magic power for good in the agricultural year to come, and the *sake*, both offered to it and heated by it, is another aspect of the meal or the food taken jointly by returning *kami* and by those who worship him.

The connection between New Year and transplanting, the most important of the agricultural tasks of the portion of the year just starting, is evident not only in the affinity if not the actual identity of the *kami* honoured at each of the two cere-monies; there is in addition a set of practices, usually occurring on the eleventh day of the New Year, to which is given the title 'paddy planting', the same as that of the June transplanting, and which cannot be understood as other than a New Year wish, an advance prayer, for a propitious and successful disposal of the vital task of rice planting. Most of these practices involve the tools of the farmer. In one form that they may take, called 'paddy throwing', the New Year's pine, taken down on the eleventh day, is set up in a dry field (a field other than paddy, that is) or in the soil that is to be used for the rice seed-beds in the coming year, and then three hoes are flung from the base of the pine. Offerings are placed at the three points where they come to ground, and, accord-ing to the order and the manner in which birds peck at these offerings, it can be divined whether the rice harvest will be early, average or late. In another instance of this eleventh day ritual centred on the farmer's implements, called the 'eleventh day season feast' or 'paddy planting', the custom was to line up the various tools of the rice crop, deck them with plants and the straw rope that is used in other contexts to indicate or to induce the presence of the *kami* or to effect purification, and to leave the tools thus until the dusk. Or the array of tools, thus decorated on the eve of the New Year, was left until the night of the eleventh of the first month—a strange reminiscence of twelfth night custom.

It is strange that most of the practices of the 'Little New Year', contrary to what might be expected in that the sphere of their observance is now in large measure restricted to rural areas, are not by nature ceremonial reminiscences or

previews of the field tasks to come or magic charms designed
to assist the planting or the harvest. The main purpose of this
group of ceremonies seems to be to prepare for the presence
of or to welcome a returning *kami*—they constitute, in fact,
a soul festival of very much the same nature as the indigenous practices of Bon, in the middle of the seventh
month, which incorporated and were in some measure
distorted by elements of the Buddhist feast of All Souls. In
'Little New Year' practices, there are also distinct traces of
purificatory rituals, designed to cleanse the community on
the eve of the dangerous period of the parting of the seasons
and in preparation for the soul festival.

The central feature of the ritual of the 'Little New Year'
is most often the bonfire on which are burnt the New Year
decorations. It goes by a variety of names which indicate its
several purposes; they range from the simple 'decoration
burning' to 'devil roasting'—the expulsion of the evil spirits
who could do harm to man and crop in the ensuing period—
and 'bird fire'; this latter derives from the custom, one of
several at 'Little New Year' in the hands of children, of
driving birds away from the community territory. When the
crops begin to ripen later in the year, birds will be one of the
sources of damage; and no doubt from the ease with which it
can be disturbed and put up, the bird has been in common
and universal use as a scapegoat; fever was banished through
the agency of a bird in Bohemia, and in Sumatra it flew off
with the curse of the barren woman.

Japan's New Year ceremonies, in addition to this bird
scaring, often include an expulsion of evil spirits (similar in
form to the summer 'driving of insects' when the crops are
blight infested) immediately prior to the New Year contest
which is the basis for divination about the state of the crops
and so must be staged in the absence of all evil influences.
This New Year devil driving is an instance of the periodic
exupulsion of evil which occurs in many other cultures at a
marked change of season. At the end of the Arctic winter,
evil spirits are driven forth at the sun's first reappearance at
Point Barrow. By the old calendrical observance, this New

Year devil drive in Japan would coincide with the opening of the spring's first plum blossom.

The fires of the 'Little New Year' are also sometimes called the 'blaze of the guardian *kami*', the tutelary *kami* of the community whose worship again often tends to be given over to the care of children. The sites connected with this guardian or barrier *kami*—the village outskirts, a prominent crossroads, the approach to a bridge, a river channel and so on, all of which offer opportunities for preventing unwelcome entry into community territory—are often the places

Effigies and birds of straw used as scapegoats are escorted off community territory as a protection against insect pest

chosen for the 'Little New Year' bonfires. Their embers are often used to toast *mochi* which is offered to the year-*kami* and then eaten by all members of the community; each household has contributed materials to build the bonfire, materials—the New Year decorations—which are thought of as being the resting place if not the transformation of the returning *kami*, so that each household by this joint banquet is doubly protected from illness for the year to come. The

D   49

power of the charm of the New Year bonfire seems to be regarded as restricted to the members of the contributing household and the house buildings themselves; its ashes spread around the outside of the walls will ward off insects—which can bite and kill or at least cause a debilitating fever—and its warmth will protect from illness for the year. In addition, if the aged smear ash from this fire over their bodies, they will regain their youth. This may perhaps have some bearing on the reason for the frequent appearance of rituals managed entirely by children at Bon as well as at the start of the New Year. Though many of these customs have degenerated now into little more than children's games and pieces of mischief, they were once all solemn rituals; it may be that, at a time when everyone added a year to his age—on New Year's Day rather than on his individual birthday—the gloom on the part of one too old to be entirely at ease at the rapid growth of the figure was magically compensated by the fact of a series of specifically child-administered ceremonies.

The embers or the ash of these bonfires should never be stepped on, nor are they ever spread on the fields as a fertilizer. In one of the few instances in which they appear to be regarded as possessed of any magic fertility capacity in connection with the crops, the householder after scattering the ashes around the outside of his home would rush with what he had left to a fruit or nut tree, brandish an axe near to its trunk and exclaim, 'Bear no fruit, and I chop'.

It seems, then, that the 'Little New Year' fires, like their counterparts exactly six months later at Bon, are best regarded as kindled to give an appropriate send-off to the *kami* at the end of their stay. There is ample evidence that the *kami*—the ancestral spirits of the household as well as the year-*kami*—are thought to return and remain for the New Year celebrations: the decorations which constitute the primary materials of these fires are the 'door pines' put up to welcome the returning spirits and thought of as their place of sojourn; and other New Year customs are best, or only, explained on the thesis that they are present or that their return is expected. One of these, *namahage*, again involves

'*Bear fruit or I chop.*' Tree threatening at Little New Year

the children—in most cases the boys only—of the community. It is usually an event of 'Little New Year's Day'. Boys and youths put on fancy dress, don devil masks and, hiding their identity in the straw coats and sandals that serve as the rain-wear of rural Japan, go the rounds of the households of the community, making a special point of seeking for mis-demeanours on the part of children or newly-married brides. (This custom is also part of the Bon ritual, six months later almost to the day, in the western districts of Kyūshū; it is yet one more instance of the similar basis of Bon and New

Namahage

Year, and here, in the seventh month, there is an interesting swing of attention on the part of the child visitors from newly weds to 'new Bon' households—houses, that is, that have suffered the death of a member since the Bon festival of the previous year.) When they come across such houses, they go through actions which mime the misconduct they have unearthed, they are given a couple of cakes of *mochi* for their pains, and they return home content.

These children's visits in disguise, originally part of a solemn ritual, have now in most instances degenerated into little beyond the children's joke. But the original intent of the disguise was to give the atmosphere of the magic or the strange; some of the children's actions are an attempt at miming a threat or a menace, others are simply those of the beggar. The various aspects of this child's ceremony all accord closely with the several stages in the development of Japanese belief in the 'guest *kami*'; originating at an early stage in Japan's past, this doctrine and the activities it promoted emphasized the magic and out of the ordinary properties of the visitor; then, at a later stage, the visiting *kami*—other than one connected with the community as a whole or one of the households within it—came to be treated as an outside beggar, the professional dropper-in, and so was ranked on the lowest rung of the *kami*-ladder.

The construction of small huts out of doors was another 'Little New Year' activity, more common in eastern Japan, organized and managed exclusively by children, though nowadays it is only very rarely practised. The children chose their own leader and began preparations as much as two weeks beforehand. The hut, made of straw—again straw as the detergent as well as the hardiest and most viable construction material—miscanthus, pine and cryptomeria branches, was festooned with the *shimenawa* rope of chastity. In the north of Japan the 'New Year Hut' was often built out of piled up snow. In some instances, the *shintai*—the '*kami*-body', the physical object, such as the mirror, into which it is believed that the *kami* has entered—was housed in this hut for the space of the festival; in others, the hut was used as the site of a vigil, undergone by the children, for several days or just the single night before the start of the festival proper. It seems then that these children's huts were another form of the temporary purification dwelling place to which were confined either those who were to be involved in gross uncleanliness—such as the woman about to begin labour or entering a menstrual period—or those who expected or hoped to be in contact with the *kami*. Their function fulfilled at the end of the preparatory vigil, the huts usually became material for the 'Little New Year' fires of the fifteenth day.

The contest, like the children's hut, common both to New Year and to Bon, is another feature of the New Year ceremonies that presupposes the belief that the *kami* are present, for the theory behind such contests is that, performed as they are before the spirits, their outcome constitutes an indication of the latters' will in the matter of the weather and the yield of the crops in the year to come. The most common form of this type of contest is the tug of war, which is fought more frequently at 'Little New Year' in the eastern part of Japan, at Bon in the west. In this, as in other aspects of the divinatory contest, the community is split and

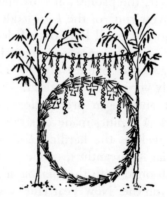

Protection throughout the second half of the year is assured by passing through a ring of reeds

the rival teams are constituted according to regional or occupational divisions. The winners—left of the river versus right of the river, for example—will enjoy the more fruitful yield. (For further discussion, see Chapter Five, Bon.)

The result of the contest fought out in the distinguished presence of the *kami* is by no means the only subject regarded as a divinatory indication at the New Year season. Weather prospects for the year to come are often gauged at the New Year by the amount of rice gruel that enters into the tube of a length of bamboo or reed placed vertically in the middle of a pan. For a preview of the whole year's weather, broken down by months, twelve beans are arranged in the ashes of the hearth; each bean represents a month and where the bean turns white, then its corresponding month will have fair weather; if the bean begins to blacken as it roasts, the month will bring heavy rain. Where a bean wheezes and hisses in the roasting, the month which it represents will be marked by high winds. Or, by a simpler method, the weather on each of the first twelve days of the New Year is taken as an indication of that of its corresponding month. To determine whether the rice crop of the year will be early, middling or late, on the eve of the New Year, or the 'Little New Year', three pieces of *mochi*, one representing each of the periods, are placed in a container filled with rice; a mortar is placed over this container and then when it is removed on the following morning, the number of rice ears adhering to each piece is counted. The greatest total indicates the season when the harvest will be ready. In one village in Gumma Prefecture, to the north-east of Tokyo, on the night before 'Little New Year', the inhabitants use an observation point by the side of a stone in the centre of the village to get a fix on the moon relative to an indicator tree on the horizon above them. If the moon is to the east of the tree, the year will be good, if to the south, bad.

The New Year fires, too, just as those that mark the end of the Bon ceremonies, often indicate the spirits' intention; they are, after all, built from the various offerings made to them, and the objects in which they have resided or with which they have had contact. And in that these fires consist of materials like door pine and vigil shelter, they signify the end of the need for excessive purificatory precaution such as is demanded immediately before and during the period of the sojourn of the *kami*. It may be, too, that this 'young' fire—the first festival bonfire of the year—can work magic and remove the years. The old men of Akita, in the north-east, certainly think so, for mere participation, even, in the final New Year rite is believed to bring all the signs of returning youth; and, as was mentioned above, for an added insurance some of them will carefully gather some of the embers, take them home, make them into a mud paste and smear it over their bodies.

One must go far in Japan to find the shrine, or even the ceremony, that does not have its fire festival. Hence the short expectation of life of practically every religious building! Hence, also, it would be mistaken to regard these New Year or winter fires as acts of sympathetic magic designed to create warmth and light to urge on the sun when it is at its weakest. The New Year fires are no different essentially from those of the rest of Japan's festival year. Fire, like salt and water, is a purifier. It removes pollution both before and after any public or private crisis. The association of fire and impurity is so intimate that the two are often used as synonyms; so, the practice of allowing the old fire to die and kindling a new one to mark the finish of a period of impurity is called, not 'pollution lifting' or 'pollution clearing', but 'fire clearing'. On New Year's Eve, the community shrine lights a huge fire in its compound; parishioners kindle torches at it, make their way home and transfer the light of the torch to the new fire in the hearth and use this to cook the rice and vegetable stew that is often the first meal of the New Year.

> The snow that lies so deep
> On this New Year's Day
> Promises a fruitful autumn.
> (*Manyōshū* xvii; 3925)

Three

BIRTHS, MARRIAGES AND DEATHS

In the private or family life of the individual, just as in the corporate life of the community, one of the most powerful springs of action is the urge to ritual purity; consequently, there are many prohibitions and taboos laid on pollution. The highlights of the community's ritual year are, by and large, the critical seasonal junctures when the spirits are present, either voluntarily or through the invocation of those who serve them. On both counts, the simple fact of the crisis, and the propinquity of the *kami*, it is imperative to purge all aspects of pollution by a series of preparatory rituals of fasting, self-denial, and positive purification. The same is the case with the life cycle of the individual or the household, for the cycle is marked by a series of crisis points —the onset of menstruation, marriage, childbirth and death; careful purificatory preparation must be made to meet these critical moments and the various pollutions and taboos which they entail are to be treated with the utmost circumspection.

But the taboos and the rituals concerning the defilements created by the crises in the individual life cycle have, if anything, suffered more than those of the community. The remote seaside village or the mountain hamlet are, naturally, more likely to preserve the longer and the more faithfully both aspects, the community and the household, of the purificatory ceremonial at the time of crisis. Yet, even so, there are many instances where the influence of the stress and bustle of modern urban life has spread beyond the city limits and has crowded out, more particularly, the observance of the private or the household ceremonies. And as for the city, although some of the community rituals are maintained—though often in drastically modified form— urban conditions and environment hardly make for the easy observance of the household ones: the girls' high school system, with its regular and testing examinations, leaves little scope for strict attention to the elaborate traditional ceremonies and restrictive taboos at the time of the onset of the girl's first menstrual period; the maternity home, the growing practice of the wife's home sewing or rudimentary secretarial job, and apartment living, with families of six or seven to a room and a toilet for every twenty rooms the norm rather than the exception, all make a nonsense of the old rules of a ritual pollution lasting thirty days or more, and a seventy or seventy-five day secular taboo on the mother after her delivery.

In rural Japan, however, many of these pollution prohibi- tions and taboos, or at least practices that arise directly from them, are still studiously observed. Sensitivity to the heinousness of uncleanliness and the consequent preservation of taboo depends on a number of varying considerations. On the whole, it seems that the farmer's awareness is consider- ably more acute than the fisherman's; perhaps the latter's constant association with the cleansing salt water makes him feel that little is needed in the way of additional precaution and prohibition. Again as a very general rule with a fair num- ber of exceptions, western Japan has tended to preserve the taboo concerned with the 'red' and the 'black' pollution more faithfully than eastern or north-eastern areas. Another factor to influence the strictness of the observance of these taboos (which may, though only in part, account for the regional divergence) concerns the religion prevailing in or the religious susceptibility, regardless of sect or creed, of an area. There are some districts, notably in the west of Japan, where just about any religion goes. Okayama Prefecture and its surroundings are one such area; another is Yamato, the district around Nara and one of the cradles of Japan's culture. This is indeed a matter of greater religious awareness in such areas, and not a mere general credulity and ready gullibility. The Japanese themselves indicate this when they describe the people of Okayama as '*kashikoi*'—cunning or acute—in business matters, and the Yamato man is by no means the soft-head who would make himself poor for his faith. Similarly, observation of the taboos entailed by the 'red' pollution has been maintained comparatively strictly in those districts where the old shrine Shintō and the comparatively new sects of Shintō have always been strong—and, in the past hundred years, both Okayama and Yamato have witnessed the birth and rapid spread of new religious faiths classed as sect Shintō and just as fully conscious as the early Shintō of the distastefulness to the *kami* of any ritual stain. Certain Buddhist sects, notably Shingon and Tendai, were from the first not unsympathetic to the ritualistic formulae of Shintō and soon tended to reinforce Shintō's emphasis on the vital importance of purification and perfection; thus, in sectors where the Shingon sect established a firm hold, such as the island of Shikoku, the ceremonial necessitated by the 'red' pollution involved in menstruation, childbirth and so on was treated no less lightly than that of the 'black' pollution of death, proper to Buddhism and either ignored or hurried over cursorily by Shintō. Yet, other sects of Buddhism, particularly the Shin branch of Pure Land Amidism, have never laid great stress on the stains of ritual uncleaniness, and in the areas where they have prevailed, such as on the northern coast of the main island, in the present-day prefectures of Fukui, Ishikawa and Niigata, attention to these prohibitions has never been the mark of strict devotion.

First, then, the 'red' pollution—the ritual uncleanliness caused by the flowing of blood at any of the crises of the life cycle, blood which is so distasteful to the *kami* that in a ritual document of the early ninth century, the use of the word itself is tabooed in connection with the most august shrines of the land, and it is decreed that the word 'perspiration' be employed in its place. The appearance of a girl's first menstrual blood is the first of these crises of the 'red' pollution. Many civilizations, particularly, it seems, those that border the Pacific, have laid prohibitions on women at their menstrual period. The Gonds, the largest aboriginal element in India, who are distributed over the central regions and the Deccan, impose a series of taboos on a menstruating woman: she should not carry water for domestic use or cook; she may not enter a cattle shed, for she pollutes animal flesh if she touches it, nor should she set foot in the fields. Her husband may enter the room where she is but may not touch her nor may he enter a temple during her period. Once the flow ceases, a bath is prepared, and after the woman has entered it and smeared powder on her body she may begin the round of her everyday domestic tasks.

The pattern of these prohibitions is fairly general and widespread. It is vital that the menstruating woman be prevented from touching and so contaminating the particular commodity or product by which the community gains its livelihood. So, in Muralug in the Torres Straits Islands, a woman must not eat any marine product in the course of her period, for the least trace of her contaminating contact would bring about the risk of the complete failure of the season's fisheries. The danger of the spread by contagion of this form of 'red' contamination as well as the scope of the actions of the menstruating woman herself are limited by confining her during the course of her period in a dark and crude menstrual hut, secluded from the other members of her community. There is also a quite widespread belief that the sun should not shine on puberty. In British Columbia the girl at the threshold of this first crisis was furnished with a wide-brimmed hat to keep off the sun's rays and was made to live alone in a dark hut for as long as two years. But a Cambodian girl, whose seclusion was often as lengthy, was allowed to move freely outside her hut at the time of a solar eclipse.

There are traces of most of these practices in early Japan. A woman diarist of the first years of the eleventh century enters this record: 'Then the expected defilement approached. Knowing I should have to leave the temple, I withdrew to a house below it. In the evenings came the booming of the great sunset bells and the hum of the cicadas.

Five days or so later, the defilement passed and I returned to the temple.' Menstruating women were often bundled off to spend their period in the parturition huts with such as were awaiting or recovering from the delivery of their child. It was particularly important to preserve the sites of the most august Shintō shrines from all taint of 'red' contamination. One such site was the shrine of the Sun Goddess at Ise, rebuilt on the same ground and to exactly the same pattern every twenty years. The rebuilding itself would eliminate a considerable amount of the stain, but, for an added insurance, all women in the shrine's vicinity about to become infected with the 'red' contamination were removed to the far side of the river that runs alongside the shrine's buildings and made to take up residence there, until they were purged, in a line of dark and dingy shacks which still stood not far short of a hundred years ago and went by the name of Delivery Row.

As in other civilizations, the Japanese sun was not allowed to shine on the 'red' pollution, or on any object that had come into contact with it. However, whereas in the practice of other peoples it seems that the prohibition arose rather from the belief that the sun's rays would do harm to the person under contamination—the Zulu, for example, thought that a woman would be shrivelled up by its light—the Japanese taboo is designed to preserve the purity of the sun, herself created through a purification ritual after her begetter, the male of the divine creators, had been in contact with the 'black' contamination.

Most of the restrictions that still remain, or were practised until comparatively recently, in connection with the impurity of menstruation, are to do with the two main ritual cleansers in Japan, water and fire. A menstrual woman may not take her usual dip in the household bath, and though the old strictness has been relaxed sufficiently for her to cook for the household, her very use of the fire renders it unclean, and once the food prepared by her while still contaminated has been consumed—it is eaten up at the end of her period—the fire is allowed to go out and a new purified fire is kindled on the following morning. It is quite common for women during their period to avoid all contact with the *kami*, to give up any form of service of the spirits, even down to the matter of the offerings on the household altar-shelf, and to steer well clear of any shrine compound. And at the end of her period, before she returns to her normal livelihood, and to signify the beginning of this return, a woman may cleanse herself by sprinkling salt over her body and clothes.

The months of pregnancy, while not notable for any significant measures to combat pollution, or prophylactics against the greatest of all the forms of 'red' pollution that is to come, yet involve some interesting instances of sympathetic magic. The pregnant woman should avoid preparing vegetables of abnormal shapes, such as the *daikon*, a type of horseradish, in case the child she is carrying be born deformed. When water is one of the ingredients of her cooking, it should always be poured into the pan before any of the other items are added; failure to observe this recipe guide for expectant cooks may well result in a dry delivery.

The first 'dog' day, one of the twelve in the Chinese cycle, in the fifth month of pregnancy (less frequently in the seventh month) marks one of the first preparations. It is the day of 'taking the band', an abdominal band of white cloth about ten feet long which ensures a safe and easy delivery. The dog has a pre-eminently easy time at whelping and it is hoped that this facility will be transmitted by the choice of the day. The dog appears again at a later stage; the character for dog may be written—it is often caked on in lipstick—on the young child's forehead at the time of its first venture out of doors. This practice the Japanese usually attempt to explain by the same reasoning, that an easy delivery is thus assured: but when the child is being hoisted on its mother's back to prepare for its first outing, it seems a little late in the day to be concerned about its safe and painless arrival. There must be some further association here, the significance of which has become lost or has been misunderstood with the passage of time, or even in the borrowing of this practice from China. For the custom of 'taking the band' has all the outward signs of Chinese origin; it is performed according to China's cyclical calendar, and during the fifth or the seventh month; an indigenous practice might have been expected to show a proper Japanese preference for the even number.

The dog is not the only animal to be involved in the practice of transfer magic. In cases where a difficult birth is expected, or where labour is unduly prolonged, a horse (which, from apparently mistaken notions about the ease with which it is delivered, is thought of as the lodging place of the deity of delivery) may be haltered and dragged up into the hills. The *kami* of delivery, like most of his kind, and especially those that deal in any aspect of production, is imagined as commuting at different seasons of the year between paddy and hill forest. But the Japanese, in these practices designed to induce magic transfers of the animals' abilities, as always, tend to look on the good side of things. By comparison, the Gonds in India take care to prevent the shadow of a horse falling on or crossing a pregnant woman, for, if this should occur, her pregnancy, like the horse's, will be dragged out to a full twelve months!

When the delivery is imminent, bundles of straw, stones, and often a broom are placed ready in the room set aside for the confinement. These objects are all in some way connected with the deity of delivery; they serve as his resting place, or are interpreted as his manifestation during his stay in the place of confinement—for he is so untypical of the *kami* species as to be able to bring himself to dwell with 'red' contamination for three, or according to some interpretations, as long as seven days! It is extremely difficult to tie down the identity of this *kami* of delivery. He cannot be identical with the *uji* deity—the *kami* of the clan or the parish—for the latter has an intense distaste for all forms of pollution, as is indicated by the many purificatory preludes to a festival in his honour, as well as by the careful removal from his service of all who are contaminated. Yet that there is some relationship between the *kami* of delivery and the *kami* of the community is indicated by the fact that the stones, which are thought of as the former's lodging place and which are placed in the confinement room at the time of the delivery and also at the side of the congratulatory rice on the tray for the offerings, are carefully picked from ground within the confines of the latter's jurisdiction. Again, the Boundary *Kami*, often confused with the *kami* of the community, is regarded as a protector of infants, and his lodging place is more often than not a natural rock or stone. Stones appear throughout Japan's history as the recipients of prayers for a safe and easy delivery, or for the grant of fertility, and as the objects of questions by parents anxious to divine the sex of their unborn child. And the stone appears as the charm facilitating delivery in the ancient practice whereby on the occasion of a pregnancy in the Imperial Household, two stones were presented to the court by the priest-in-charge of the Shrine of Aso in Kyūshū, which nestles under the volcano of that name still today spasmodically active.

A further site of the *kami* of delivery's lodging place during the confinement is the broom. Hence the presence of the broom among the articles prepared before delivery. The broom has other magic properties; if stood the wrong way up, it will remove guests who have outstayed their welcome. In the Aso area, it is set up, again upside down, by the feet of a woman in labour, or used to massage her stomach in the event of protracted labour. This is probably the significance of the straw in the list of essential labour-room equipment, for straw is one of the materials that go to make a broom and there are, in fact, instances of the use of this straw, tied into a bundle, to sweep away the taint of the 'red' contamination from the altar-shelves of the house at the close of the period of pollution engendered by the confinement. This veneration of the broom—it should on no account be stepped on—may have developed from a symbolic interpretation of its movements when in use; it may push away (as it does in the case of the dull guest) or it may pull inwards and so attract (as it may perhaps do in the case of the deity of delivery). Or, and this appears the more likely explanation, the respect in which the broom is held may derive from the magic play on words of which the Japanese is so fond. One ancient name for the broom was *hahaki* a word which is identical in sound with 'mother wood' or 'life-giving tree'. In this case, it is not unnatural to regard the broom as the manifestation of the deity of delivery and to worship it as such—and there are many districts where the broom is offered sacred *sake* in celebration of a safe delivery.

That the delivery deity is sometimes imagined as residing in the hills is already clear from the practice of leading a horse into the hills to meet and escort the deity in instances where labour is protracted. In parts of the Tōhoku area this notion concerning residence is intensified to become a belief in the identity of the two—mountain and delivery *kami*. The motive for this kind of identification is not clear, although the mountain deity is often conceived of as female and as giving birth herself to twelve children in the year. Certainly, it would be a gain to have such fecundity and first-hand experience present at any delivery. Thus, again in this area, the usual habit is to repair to the mountains and to escort the mountain *kami* to the place of confinement as soon as it appears that labour is established. Nor does this *kami* allow its presence to go unnoted: the feeling of heaviness in the back that often occurs just before the delivery itself is accounted for by the explanation that it is the full weight of the mountain deity standing there to lend assistance.

Parturition huts of the kind that used to form Delivery Row over the river from the Sun Goddess's Shrine at Ise have existed from the earliest days. Their purpose was to localize and to remove from the normal spheres of common activity all taint of the contamination of delivery. They no doubt derive from the period when the clan was closely-knit and living was common, with the clan as the unit. The period of confinement within the hut was normally governed by the length of time stipulated before the mother and her baby reached the stage of secular purity—normally thirty days or more after the delivery. Parturition huts were sometimes thatched with feathers of the cormorant, as a fertility symbol.

There are nowadays no known instances of the practice of condemning a woman about to enter labour to a delivery hut, and there is little attempt, from the secular aspect at least, at cutting her off and limiting the extent of the pollution she engenders, beyond setting aside a room for the delivery and stipulating who is allowed to enter and at what stage after the birth such comings and goings become permissible. But from the ritual and religious aspect more thorough-going precautions are sometimes still observed. As a prelude to the Great Purification, a ritual which precedes the festival of Hachiman on an island off the western tip of the main island, all members of households where during the past year there has been any calamity resulting from either 'red' or 'black' contamination are taken to the peak of the island's hill, and are confined there until the festival is over.

There is a variety of charms to assist the delivery itself and to ensure that no complications develop immediately afterwards. Many of these are food charms; one edible fern not only helps to eliminate the prospects of a difficult delivery, but also ensures the health and strength of the child after birth; it is, in fact, a multi-purpose preventative effective also in the event of an incidence of the 'black' pollution, for it assists escape from the consequences of contamination by contact with death. Where the supply of milk is insufficient or where milk has not even begun to flow to the breasts, transfer magic is often called into play. The gingko tree has sack-like growths which drip after rain like over-full breasts. This deposit is caught in a cup and drunk, in the hope that the potion will induce breasts as distended as the tree's.

In communities close to the sea, or where the sea plays a vital part in the local livelihood, the relation of the time of birth to the state of the tide is of deep significance. A child born with the tide at the full or on the rise will live; a birth when the tide is at its lowest or is on the ebb is of ill omen, and the child's chances of survival are rated very low. This is another instance of the Japanese predilection for the full and the perfect, and of the distaste found in decay. There seems

66

to be no tradition in rural areas of a correlated almanac calculated according to the stage of the moon.

There are many practices connected with the dispersal of the after-birth and the equipment used during labour. The umbilical cord is wrapped in paper, the day, month and year of birth are written on it and it is preserved against the time when the child encounters a critical illness. If at such time it is broiled and the liquid distilled from it is drunk, recovery will be rapid. A girl whose umbilical cord has not been used in this way takes it with her as a bride to her new home and at her death it is placed at her side in the coffin.

The after-birth is best buried in a place where no one will step over it. As it is imagined that when the child grows, it will suffer from an ineffaceable horror of the animal that first steps on the after-birth—it might be a cat, a snake, a rat or a repulsive insect of the kind that Japanese houses seem to breed so well—it is the custom for the father to take one ceremonial step over the spot after he has filled in the soil. A further practice is to dispose of the after-birth of a male child just inside the limits of the household compound, and that of a girl just outside them; as a result, the boy will remain always as a member of the household and bring it prosperity, the girl will marry and depart from the house of her birth.

There are different ideas about the length of the delivery deity's stay with the mother and new-born child. In some areas, the straw bed prepared as the deity's resting place is removed on the third day after the delivery, while in other parts, and particularly in Shikoku, the farewell ceremony does not take place until the seventh night. However, each of these limits is clearly not unconnected with other events and ceremonies. The third is the day when, in some circles, it is thought that the contamination will have dispersed enough for the new father to take his place alongside the other fisher-men or farmers in his community. It may be that it is imagined that this deity of delivery, so untypically and insensitively involved in pollution, takes away with him (or her) the most offensive and harmful stains. On the other hand, while his departure marks a stage in the cleansing process, it also robs the child of his protection: to compensate, the child is often given a temporary name which it bears for four days until the next well-marked limit in its progress towards ritual cleanliness. To have no name would invite every kind of calamity.

The seventh day is marked by similar ceremonies and relaxations of taboos. On this day, men are permitted to enter the confinement room; this is again consistent with the belief in some quarters that the delivery deity remains with its charges until the seventh day. In some areas, it is customary for the mother now to get up for the first time, and the seventh day naming ceremony is a nationwide practice. The infant is dressed in its best clothes and offerings of congratulatory rice, or of rice flour moulded into the shape of fish, pine, or plum (all emblems of long or flourishing life) are made. So the departure of the guardian delivery deity is again a sign both for ceremonies designed to ensure compensatory precautions and for another advance towards a state of freedom from contamination.

In some instances the mother is allowed to return to her normal household life on the seventh day. But this is considerably earlier than usual, for the most widely practised custom is that on the fifteenth day she purifies herself—she washes her hands thoroughly if no more—and then returns to routine. She may now bathe in the same water as the rest of the household, and the usage whereby she has had her food cooked at a separate fire ceases. But in more strict communities her contamination may be regarded as lasting a great deal longer; some areas of Yamato to this day demand a thirty-day isolation of the mother, and only then is she treated as pure for secular purposes. It is the practice sometimes for the mother to cover her head with a towel or a length of cloth whenever she goes out of doors before her purification is attained. The child is often similarly covered, and any washing belonging to either mother or child may often be hung under the house eaves, not directly in the sun's light. Thus is the sun's purity guarded.

The final stage in the mother's progress towards complete decontamination comes with her re-entry into ritual celebrations. Though the date varies considerably, it frequently coincides with the day for her child's first visit to the community shrine and its recognition as a member of the parish. But where the mother is still tarnished—as in parts of Yamato, for example, where the child's first visit of worship is on its eleventh day, and the mother remains ritually unclean until the seventy-fifth day after her delivery—the child, dressed in its best and with lucky charms dangling from its clothes and from the quilt-like outer coverlet over its back, is taken to the shrine on the shoulders of an elderly female relative or the midwife who assisted at the delivery. The child's face is made-up with powder, rouge and lipstick, and on its forehead, again in lipstick, is daubed the character for 'great' if it be a boy, if a girl, that for 'small'.

The age at which the child makes this first outing after the resolution of the taboos laid on it varies considerably: it may be as little as twenty-one days, or as many as seventy-five or even 110 or 120 days. The most usual seems to have been just over a month after the birth, the boy going on his thirty-first day, the girl on her thirty-third. The boy reaches a stage of purity that renders him acceptable to the community deity earlier than the girl; even when the date of the first presentation at the shrine exceeds a hundred days from birth, the boy's visit occurs ten days before the girl's which falls on the 120th day. The reason for this may lie in the consideration that the girl is fated for much of her life to be involved in a greater degree of 'red' pollution.

Furnished with a name and recognized by the tutelary parish *kami*, the child is now doubly protected against the many dangers that assail it. Before the first presentation at the local shrine these evil influences were too oppressive for the child to be taken across a river or over any stretch of water with any safety, or even, in some instances, for it to be lifted up and carried on the back. There is sometimes a reminiscence of this safeguard in the case of animals; on the third day after its birth, a calf or a foal may be given a name and be made to step through a shallow pool of water slopped over the paddock.

Fire is the most effective detergent, and thus the need to preserve its purity is a matter of utmost urgency. So it is with a 'fire-changing' ceremony, in which the old unclean fire is put out and a new pure fire is lit, that the 'red' pollution of birth is finally purged. And it may be because of this care at all costs to prevent a spread of the contamination to another household that in some villages along the shore of Lake Biwa anyone from a family where there has been a birth will refrain for a whole year from taking a light for his tobacco from every fire but his own.

The time of marriage is the next crisis in the life cycle. The simple ceremony based on three sips from three *sake* cups may hide a magic play on words, for although again the appearance of the odd number in this type of ritual ceremony is strangely un-Japanese, 'three-three', *san-san*, could also mean 'birth after birth' and fill the function of a fertility charm. There are often similar hints at expectations that the union will prove fertile in the banquet that follows the ceremony. In some districts the lads of the village will haul into the banquet room a stone statue of Jizō, the child's guardian deity, the shape of which often has more than a gentle suggestion of phallic symbolism. The statue is placed before the bride, she makes offerings to it—sometimes presenting it with a new bib—and it is then returned to its proper place, usually near the community boundaries as an auxiliary tutelary spirit.

As the bride leaves her parents' household to set off for her new home, a small fire of rice straw is often lit in the court-yard. A similar fire is kindled as the coffin leaves the house for the last journey of the dead. The bride is now virtually dead to the house of her birth; yet the ceremony of mar-riage is not considered complete until she has made a ritual return there, usually on the third day after the wedding. Formerly, during the wedding procession the bride was frequently the target of handfuls of dirt thrown by her un-married male contemporaries. This practice has been interpreted as a means of ensuring that the new wife takes some of her native soil with her to her fresh home; but anger and jealousy, of old friends who are losing a prize to a rival of another community, seem to furnish more satisfactory motives.

The consummation of marriage involves the stains of 'red' pollution. Anciently, in addition to the confinement huts where women in childbirth and sometimes those entering a menstrual period were shut off, there were also nuptial huts, set apart from the dwelling area of the community, so that the latter might not be involved in the blood-letting of lost virginity. Because of his involvement in this uncleanliness, the newly-wed male is sometimes avoided by his fellows for three days after his marriage and, in certain fishing communities, is prohibited from going on board his ship and taking part in joint fishing operations for a similar period.

Because of the decay and dissolution that follow it, death has from the earliest times been distasteful to the Japanese. Where the 'black' pollution assails, there is no longer the promise of life and growth that is the feature of every instance of the incidence of 'red' contamination. Thus, although the latter is the more damaging if not contained and purged, it is of much more moment that its contamination be removed. Where the dread of the 'red' is tinged with life, the revulsion for the 'black' bears in itself no compensations. However, the precautions demanded by the 'black' pollution are best taken as speedily as may be, before the decay commences to eat in. Then, neglect and dismissal from the mind; and the Japanese is well skilled at bringing himself to ignore what he wishes to be ignored. Hence, the tomb, the resting place of the decaying body, is soon forgotten and hence also, the contamination of the 'black' pollution is sooner dispersed than that of the 'red'.

As with most ritual celebrations, standards are failing; both the scope of a taboo and the period of time for which it is observed have been reduced considerably. In one fishing village the whole community was affected for three days until the early 1920s; the children of the deceased were laid under taboos for fifty days, and other family members were regarded as contaminated for periods which varied with the closeness of their relationship. Now, only the family and those from the community who assist in the many tasks prior to and connected with the funeral are regarded as affected, and they only for a mere three days. However, there still remain areas where the old traditions are given some recognition. A village on the shores of Lake Biwa (where those affected by a birth never lit their tobacco from another's fire) regards the incidence of a death within its boundaries as involving enough pollution to prohibit every member of the community from entering the compound of the parish shrine for seven days. And the same sort of caution, though less drastic, against the spread of uncleanliness in ritual matters is shown in another village, a little further to the east, where a measure of rice is contributed by each household to make up the offerings for the annual festival of the parish deity, and where the rice contributed by those families that have suffered a death during the year since the last celebration of the festival is collected and stored in a separate sack.

When the coffin leaves the house after the funeral service, straw matting is thrown over the spot where it lay and the floor is swept with a bundle of straw. Straw seems to be regarded as having considerable purificatory powers; it is put in the confinement room when the woman goes into labour not only as a resting place for the deity of delivery but in addition to help in dispersing the contamination with which this deity must be riddled; and, after all, straw is almost always one of the primary components of the cleansing fire. As in the case of the bridal procession, a straw fire is lit at the gate after the coffin and its retinue have passed, and a dish or cup that belonged to the deceased is broken; this may be to signify the final severing of his link with the home, or it is occasionally interpreted as the third calamity in succession (in addition to death and fire—the straw kindled at the gate) which should complete the series. Then, to erase all traces of the footmarks of the cortege so that the spirit of the dead, which could be malicious, might not find its way back, and again to remove the pollution left where the coffin has passed, the ground of the courtyard is given a thorough sweeping.

During the funeral period there are several instances where actions are performed in the exact reverse of usual practice. The screen in the room by the corpse is often inverted, and the hanging scroll in the alcove may be turned so that the picture faces the wall. Chopsticks usually laid flat on a tray beside the bowl of rice are placed vertically in the bowl, and where water is used, it is ladled with a backhand instead of the normal forehand movement. There are several such conventions involving the clothes of the dead person; his *kimono* is folded with the left side uppermost, his sash is tied with a granny knot and if his clothes are later hung out to air, they are inside out. When the body lies in state, it is placed in such a position that the head rests on a 'north pillow'—the crown of the head, that is, facing north.

'Black' pollution clings to the deceased's close relatives for forty-nine days. Anciently, this period or at least a part of it was spent in a mourning hut, akin to the confinement hut, built near the tomb. Some areas adhered to this practice until the early years of this century, and there is clearly a relic of it in the custom, still occasionally followed today, of putting up over the grave a small wooden structure shaped like a house and called a 'soul house'.

Although the period of death taboos is not long, the extent of these taboos is considerably wide. The pollution of death is often thought to extend to friends and neighbours of the same age as the dead person who resort to a variety of methods of altering their years and so of avoiding the calamity that threatens them. Any animals or household pets that belonged to the dead man are also liable to pollution, so that, to escape danger, a horse or a cow may be exchanged temporarily or may change hands through a bogus bill of sale. In this instance can be seen the difference of the degree of dread with which the 'red' and the 'black' pollutions are viewed; the dangers involved in taking over a 'red'-infected animal would be too dire to allow of a trick of this nature.

All the tools and household implements in the home of the dead may be contaminated, as is the fire which is allowed to die out and is then re-lit after the rituals of the funeral are completed, in most cases three days after death.

Anyone who has had contact with death, even a member of the community funeral association who might merely have helped to serve the funeral breakfast, had best keep well away from any field where crops are growing. It is still widely thought in the Tōhoku district that the presence of a polluted person will cause the crops to wither. Nor should the person thus contaminated go out in a fishing boat or take part in any joint enterprise such as the repair of the community road or irrigation system. All matters to do with the *kami* are taboo in some communities, as is the use of a needle or climbing up the hills or mountains in village territory (such being both the home, for part of the year, of the local guardian *kami* and also the site of lumber work which often helps out the meagre existence to be had from the plain paddies). Occasionally, a woman defiled by death pollution will cover her head when she walks in the sun just as she may if involved in the impurity of birth.

Thus, each of the crises in the life cycle brings its pollution and its calamity for the individual. The primary aim was, and still is in many instances, to contain this contamination within as narrow scope as may be, and then to approach the *kami* as soon as it was dispersed. Here, the case is rather different with the critical junctures in the year cycle for the community as a whole, for though the latter are just as perilous as the calamitous moments of the individual's life, and so are most safely confronted by a ritually purified community, they do not carry contamination within themselves; so they may be met not only by a cleansed community, but even by a community buttressed by the presence of its *kami*, summoned and escorted to his shrine ready for one of the fixed year-round festivals, or on hand in an emergency through the agency of a *komori* undertaken by his parishioners.

One feature of modern Japanese life seems to have succeeded in creating something of a synthesis out of these two quite separate modes of handling crisis, that of the community and that of the individual. This feature is the examination system. One Shintō shrine, at the time of Japan's equivalent of the eleven-plus, encourages its parishioners to undertake a *komori* on behalf of their examinee children. Thus you have the sight of a hundred or more mothers, each performing an individual *komori* for an individual or a household crisis, though the nature of the crisis itself, by the absence of inherent pollution, is more akin to that facing the community at dangerous junctures in its agricultural year. In fact, this maternal *komori* practice is by no means a bad one; for, like their English counterparts, Japanese mothers tend to worry about examination success far more than do their sons and daughters.

Four

GION FESTIVAL

Kon chiki chin
Kon kon chiki chin
Kon chiki chin

This is how the man of Kyōto puts into words the shrill beat of the cymbal-gongs that rings through the Gion Festival, the highlight of Kyōto's full festival year. The gongs are shaped in a circle, and a lip runs round their circumference. They are held triangle-like and struck with a metal-tipped drumstick. *'Kon'* is a full bang, on centre; *'chiki'* is the stick moving rapidly up and down and striking the upper and lower lip; *'chin'* is another centre beat, followed by a rest. The whole tenor of the festival is set by the gay and cheeky lilt of the gong's rhythm; its piercing ring dins in your ears, sets your feet moving and your body swaying and emerges high and clear through the notes of the rest of the musicians—whether they bang away on their drums or puff red-cheeked into their flutes—and the jumble of noises from the crowd down below. Japan has a wealth of sound, and her people are quick to appreciate it; it makes them write phrases like 'bee-loud summer afternoon'. But Kyōto's Gion Festival must be one of the richest collections of them all.

The musicians sit or kneel on a platform at the top of a tall float built in the shape of a square tower mounted on a wheeled platform. Perched precariously thirty feet or more above ground, they barely have room to lift themselves to their full height and must stoop when they move across their narrow platform. They all wear the white and blue cotton *kimono* of the summer, but this is one with a difference, for the blue pattern is made up of the crest of the Gion Shrine. From the four corners of their ceiling a high roof sweeps upward. Its slope is steep and it tapers sharply. From its pointed pinnacle, there rises, for another fifteen feet or so, a single mast in the shape of a spear shaft; its tip bears a branch of the sacred *sakaki* tree, green and lifelike as ever in the still air of the baking July heat. Again with Gion's blue crest decking their white *kimono*, and with grimy greasy sweatbands knotted at their foreheads below their dank hair, four men cling frantically to their post at each corner of the base of the roof. From time to time throwing caution to the winds, they loosen their clutch on the roof with one hand which gropes in the folds of their *kimono* and brings out an object looking like a truncheon of tightly bound bamboo leaves. Inside them, there is a rice dumpling. They lean inwards to steady their weight against the roof's slope, lift their arm slowly back and hurl the truncheon. There is a surge of outstretched hands down below and a frantic scramble to catch the object as it falls. It brings good luck and good health—the latter in particular—for the whole year until the next Gion day if you manage to snatch one of these *chimaki* and hang it under the eaves, above the lintel of your front doorway.

Below the musician's platform on each face of the square tower hangs a richly woven tapestry. Blues and reds from the boldly-executed large-scale design catch your eye. Just to the west of the Gion Shrine lies the area where Kyōto's best brocade is sold, and Kyōto's is the best throughout Japan. To the west again is one of the oldest weaving districts; and among Gion's parishioner's are some of Japan's top-flight *geisha* who know all the tricks of wearing this silk. The cloth and silk trade forms the backbone of the wealth of a good many of Gion's parishioners, whose money goes unstintingly, in the best tradition of Japan's merchants of the early days, to make their festival one of the most sumptuous and spectacular in the land.

The platform on which the tower is built rests on four

huge wooden wheels, eight feet in diameter. They creak and grate on their wooden axles so noisily that you wince. Strung out along a heavy shaft that was once the trunk of a massive tree and has since suffered little from the plane are fifty of Gion's parishioners. Another fifty line two tow-ropes leading forward from the corners of the platform. Their *kimono* hem is belted in at the sash so that their calves are bared and their legs are free to move as they sweat and strain to urge on their ponderous load. Whenever they halt along the procession route—and such halts are not infrequent—the floats are urged on by two men above them. These wear the formal *hakama*, a divided skirt, and stand on the platform in front of the tower. In one hand, they hold broad white fans with a vivid red design in the centre, and with the other they clasp a rope which hangs from the upper part of the tower. As the float stops, they lean forward, almost at an angle of forty-five degrees, their weight taken by the hand holding the rope, and with wide, impelling sweeps of the fan, interspersed with perfectly synchronized ritual hand movements, they urge on the float.

Such halts are numerous, for the route of the procession is a long one, encompassing almost all the central area of the old capital. Every corner entails a long delay, for each of the twenty floats in the parade must stop, gradually edge its way to face the new line of progress as its wheels are chocked and hauled manfully round and then wait in line for the final tower to catch up. The heat is intense for this is the hottest part of Kyōto's hot and steamy summer and it is a rare Gion day when the sun is hidden by the clouds or the breeze is strong enough to stir the streamers at the summit of the float's mast. Down below on the streets, in every window of the shops and houses that line the route, the crowd jostle and strain to see the sights. And crowds there are, for some have come from either end of Japan to watch this parade, and Kyōto people themselves drop anything on hand and take the day off. Gion day, July 17th, is even a local Bank Holiday; but it gives small respite for most bank employees, and managers in fact, for they merely exchange *soroban* for camera or festival handbook. They see as many clients—and more—as on the average Friday, for the route of the parade seems almost to have been planned of set purpose to take in every central bank building; staff and manager are at work at eight in the morning, shepherding their clients to their seats on the trestled and terraced platform on the pavement before the bank.

There are others who work just as hard on this day of festivity; and none harder than the maintenance men of the city transport department. For almost the whole of its course, the parade passes along streets where there is a tram route. So, an hour or so before the procession is due to pass, they begin to dismantle the overhead wires, shinning up the cable poles which clutter the skyline in any Japanese town and either become the central feature of the schoolboy painting or make a mockery of nearly every deliberately positioned photograph. Then, almost as the last of the floats makes its slow and laboured turn into the next road on its route, up go the cables again, and on come the trams, drivers chafing at lost schedules and stepping savagely and almost continuously on their hooter pedals. The blare of the hooters adds to the din, but clear and piercing above it all comes

Kon kon chiki chin

The lilt is steady, the tempo constant, almost halting at times in its constancy. But the musicians are really in the mood now; the beats are automatic, yet there is a frenzy in them, the frenzy of weariness and weariness conquered; for the musicians have not slept a wink on the previous night. They have spent it on their platforms in the floats, lining Shijō, Fourth Street, the broadest and busiest of the ten or more east-west streets in Kyōto's chequer-board layout. And through the night, they have steadily and relentlessly beaten out their tune, *Kon chiki chin*. . . .

Gion festival is typical of the urban summer *matsuri* in Japan. Noise, bustle and lavish decoration are its prime features; the procession of floats, the use of an orchestra to give musical accompaniment to many of the rituals that go with it and the carrying of the *mikoshi* (the portable ark for the *kami*) around the confines of the parish are the main elements of the ritual. All this rowdy activity, the very fact of the procession even, is in marked contrast to the long tradition of the *matsuri* in honour of the clan or local tutelary *kami* which is at the base of Japanese festival celebration. In the latter case, the festival formula has at its heart the solemn and quiet joint feast with the deity, a feast preceded by a purification ceremony and the escorting of the *kami* to the site of the festival, and followed by the departure of the *kami* and the ceremonies that adorn it. But Gion's din and bustle are contagious and there is many a village parish-deity ceremony which has imported at least one of its elements, be it either procession, gong, or the passage of the *mikoshi*.

There is a deal of truth in the generalization that while by its nature the spring or autumn festival fits the countryside, the summer festival is of the town. For while the former are almost exclusively concerned with the agricultural year and mark its start and finish, the summer festival, broadly, deals in conflagrations, epidemics and the like, the calamities that the city can only or can best produce. In fact, all the notable summer festivals practised today were born in an urban environment and in circumstances which the growth of city or capital life created. When these festivals became annual affairs, the circumstances of their origin was not forgotten. Looked at in general, they are concerned with all the calamities that Japan's (and especially western Japan's, where most of them began) hot muggy summer may bring. In addition, as positive purificatory rituals—water and, to a lesser degree, fire are often salient features—they prepare the way for the return of the ancestral spirits at Bon; and here, one is reminded of the phrase of the Kyōto man, always on the look-out for a festival to while away the heat, 'When Gion ends, Bon begins'.

For a better understanding of the circumstances that gave rise to the ceremonies that were later to develop into Gion's and other similar city summer festivals, we must go back to

Kyōto's early days. Kyōto was founded in AD 794, with the capital of China, Ch'ang-an, as its model. You can still readily discern the chequer-board plan of its centre sector; ten streets, numbered consecutively, run east-west and are crossed by a smaller number of what are now broad boulevards leading north-south. So faithful to the plan was the execution that even today, addresses are given in the form 'west of the Fourth Street—River Bank Road Intersection', or 'going upwards (i.e. north) from the junction of Temple Road and Third Street'; and the divisions of its central block are marked by names such as 'Left Capital'—the eastern sector, that is—and 'Right Capital', the west, since you turn your back to the ill-omened north.

In the period immediately following its foundation, the built-up area in the Left Capital, the eastern sector, grew very rapidly, whereas in the western half of the central area, the round-the-year dampness of the low-lying land did little to encourage swift development. Of the land most in demand for building plots, that part of the eastern sector north of Shijō, Fourth Street—the site of Gion Shrine—was especially sought after; and above it, the spur of high land which flanks Kyōto on the east became the fashionable spot for spacious and sumptuous villas. With such development going on apace, there was urgent need of great quantities of timber. Little control was exercised by the Court and as a result much of the necessary lumber was taken from the forests to the north around the head waters of the Kamo River—the Wild Duck River—where not only was the site easy to work, but where the matter of transport presented the least problems. As a result, the Kamo was rendered more prone to flooding after heavy rains; and the summer evening storm in Kyōto, though it may not last long, is liable to unleash a very considerable torrent of rain. And as the depredations grew, so did the frequency and the extent of the floods they caused increase, for it is evident from contemporary records that the Kamo river overflowed its banks more often and with ever-growing disaster from about the middle and through to the end of the Heian period—the era which took

its name from that of Kyōto at the time, the Capital of Peace.
Nor was deforestation in the wooded hill country to the
north the sole cause of Kyōto's flood calamities. The very
nature of the course of the Kamo itself was a powerful
contributory factor. Nowadays, the Kamo flows due north
south through the eastern sector of the central square of
Kyōto; but its natural course, at the time of this development and building activity, was considerably to the west, not
far from the present bed of the Hori River. The two rivers
ran close together near the point of their entry into Kyōto
proper and this fact coupled with the natural slope of the
site away from the high ground in the east and north to the
low-lying swamp lands of the west and south made the area
hardly suitable, as it was, for the full-scale development that
was envisaged. So a channel was cut into the upper stream of
the Hori and part of its flow was led off further to the east,
almost at the foot of the slopes that rose to form the eastern
spur with its highly desirable plots for select villas. This
channel, carefully banked and buttressed with firm dykes,
became the new course of the Kamo. But the enforced
changes were far from successful and in fact only increased
the dangers of flooding after a period of heavy rain. To this
day, though its channel is cut deep and though there is considerable work throughout the year on both channel and
supporting dykes, the muddy and swirling waters of the
Kamo present a very live threat after the heavy falls of
either June's 'plum rains' or September's typhoon down-
pours. There are still evident today traces of all this construction work in the place-names of the north-east limits of
the city proper; east to west through this section runs a
street the name of which might be paraphrased as 'Where the
River Now Flows Out'; and in the same district there is a
place called 'Water Coming Out'.

Most of the capital for these costly preparations for city
development was provided by the house whose clan deity
was worshipped at a shrine very close to if not at the same
spot as that which was soon to become Gion. So what more
natural, when these vast public works brought their floods

and these on top of the normal unhealthy damp of Kyōto's summer brought epidemics, than that Kyōto's ailing people should turn to this clan and its deity for assistance in banishing the evil spirit of the pestilence?

There are downright contradictions in the various traditions concerning the origin of the Gion Shrine. One popular version has it that the shrine was founded in AD 876; another consecration date is 926. Yet there seems no reason to doubt the entry in the Gion Shrine records telling of the circumstances of the first celebration of the festival in 869.

From the details of the account in these records, it appears quite certain that, at the time of the first celebration of the ceremony in 869, the priest in charge was acting as the official at the head of an established shrine, rather than that, as popular tradition would have it, the shrine was consecrated several years after the first celebration of the festival on record, either as a result of the people's gratitude or official recognition for the benefits that this ceremony had brought. This interpretation, that the shrine existed prior to the ceremony for which it became famous, is supported by the siting of the shrine building itself. Gion's main hall and ceremonial gateway face south. There is nothing unusual in this, for the north is, in general, the direction of ill omen (the corpse lies in state with the head resting on a 'north pillow'), and the north, for Kyōto, brought not only flood waters but cold and penetrating winter winds from the snow-laden mountains. On the other hand, if the shrine was built specifically to commemorate the efficacy of a priest's measures to counter an epidemic and to provide a useful bulwark against any future attacks by the plague, it should properly have faced the city and the people it was designed to protect, its hall and gate looking not so much south as west.

It would appear, then, that there was some foundation on the site of the Gion Shrine even before Kyōto became the capital. If this was so, it is easy to see the process by which a foundation which was, in the first place, the site of worship of a clan deity later developed to become the centre of rituals designed to assuage the savagery of the angry spirit of epidemics. Changes of this order are by no means unusual in the history of Japanese shrines. So what may perhaps have been the shrine of the tutelary *kami* of the Yasaka clan (once very flourishing but already by just after the middle years of the eighth century—before the move of the capital from Nara to Kyōto, in fact—considerably reduced in authority so that its members were content with lowly offices), lost its connection with the clan as the latter's influence waned and became a site for worship designed to humour the angry spirit of Susa-no-o; then, with the introduction and spread of alien elements from China and India, there was an additional swing to the identification of the shrine's patron deity as Gozu Tennō who soon assumed the specialized function of and capacity of becalming the horde of angry spirits of summer pestilences. In this sense, the tradition of connection with Susa-no-o is not inappropriate, for this *kami* was born like the Sun Goddess out of purification, since the creation story has it that he was produced from the nose of the male of the divine creator couple on his return from his visit to the female in the decaying 'Land of Darkness'. Susa-no-o, born from the nose and, in the creation story, the most unruly of the host of the *kami*, is, according to the most satisfactory of a number of interpretations, the *kami* of the hot and damp summer wind which blows all the bodily ills of summer before it.

However, rain was the principal creator of the calamities against which the Gion Shrine in its later, and present, aspect was considered effective. It may be that not only the Gion Shrine itself, but the whole area of the Shrine buildings and related or in some way connected foundations also were regarded as possessed of Gion's magic influence. Just to the west of the Gion Shrine, there is a stone statue of the *Meyami Jizō*, the 'Eye-Sickness Jizō'. Now, it may well be that, at some stage in its long history, the name of the statue has lost an initial 'a' and that the true name of the statue was, at its origin, *Ameyami*—'Rain-Stopping'. Jizō, as will be seen later, has always been and is still closely connected with rituals designed to produce rain; and from the frequency with which exactly antithetical capacities are thought to blend in a single *kami*, it seems fair to suppose that Jizō was conceived of as a rain-stopper as well as a rain-maker. Certainly a foundation called Shinsenen, Garden of the Spirit Stream, which from its early years has had close connections with the Gion Shrine—so close in fact as to lead even to this foundation putting in a rival claim to the first patronage of the ceremony designed to drive out the epidemic—has always been considered as one of the most appropriate and effective shrines to sponsor a request either for a fall of rain to break a drought, or for a cessation of the downpour in the event of floods.

According to Gion Shrine tradition, an epidemic was raging over the whole of Japan in the summer months of 869. On the seventh day of the sixth month (according to the old lunar calendar) a ceremony was held at the Shrine to stay this epidemic: in the course of this ritual, sixty-six spears were set up, designed to ward off the plague from each of the sixty-six administrative divisions into which Japan was divided at the time. Then, the *mikoshi*, the portable ark, was brought out by the boys of Kyōto, carried from the Shrine to Shinsenen, the Garden of the Spirit Stream, where another ceremony was held to exorcize the angry spirit of the epidemic, and then returned to the Shrine.

All the elements of this first celebration of the Gion ceremony, however modified or transformed, reappear in the present-day festival, as do most of the significant and distinguishing features of the typical summer festival. The site of the latter is never very far away from some aspect of water, be it the sea, a river, or merely a small pond; in much the same way, there is a tendency for the spring group of festivals to be celebrated at or near the base of a mountain. The proximity of water is another indication of the basic and common function of the summer festival, the removal of some form of uncleanliness; here, a state of purification, a banishing of pollution is the final goal, not the essential prerequisite as in the case of most of the country festivals that have to do with the year-round tasks of the field. So, Gion's ceremonies begin with a ceremonial cleansing of all the paraphernalia, the *mikoshi*, the floats and so on, as well as all the personalities concerned. This preparatory ritual is performed, appropriately, in the deeply-hollowed bed of the River Kamo, close by the stone statue of the 'Rain-Stopping' Jizō. It occurs on July 7th, the sixth month by the lunar count.

Nor is Gion Shrine's *kami* unconnected with water in the beliefs that have surrounded him as the faith in his ability to staunch the flow of summer evils has spread across Japan. Although from the earliest times the people of Kyōto regarded him as especially competent in the matter of epidemics, there is many a village where *Gion San* is worshipped as a water-deity, and is invoked when a long period of drought brings the hazard of crop-failure.

The close relationship of the summer festival with water is particularly evident in both the very nature and function of the *mikoshi* and the various rituals in which it figures. There are several technical terms to do with these rituals. The *mikoshi* may do a 'crossing'—it may be carried across water, that is, and there are not a few summer festivals in which the passage of the *mikoshi* down river, mounted on a boat, is one of the main features, if not the central one, of the whole celebration. Another of these terms, 'beach descending' again has to do with the ceremonial washing of the *mikoshi* to ensure purity preparatory to the performance of the ritual of the festival proper. It is significant that this same term 'beach descending' is used in some districts of the purificatory immersion in the sea still regarded in a few fishing communities as essential for the new mother before she is thought of as purged of the 'red' pollution involved in her delivery and fit to take her place and perform her usual duties in the household. As the home, for at least a part of the festival, of the patron deity of a shrine such as Gion where there is specialization in the matter of the function and the efficacy of the *kami*, the *mikoshi* becomes the centre of attention when thoughts turn, as they do so readily in Japan—to the question of cleansing ritually all the celebrants of a ceremony. The cleansing of the *mikoshi* is a means of purifying all who will be involved in the subsequent festival. Hence, this action fulfils the function of the *komori*, the purifying vigil preparatory to the escorting of the tutelary *kami* to his shrine home, in the clan or parish deity type *matsuri*. *Komori* and *mikoshi*-cleansing both purify the community.

Although the *mikoshi* now appears in and is an integral part of the ceremonies of many festivals of the parish *kami* type, it owes its origin to the other type of *matsuri* concerned with the expulsion of summer evils, for a text of the early years of the Heian period records an order for the construction of two *mikoshi* to be used to assist in assuaging an epidemic. During the period while the *mikoshi* is taken in riotous and unruly procession through the shrine's parish, it is the dwelling place, if not the transformed manifestation—the 'spirit body' as the Japanese put it—of the shrine's *kami*. One description of it still heard occasionally is 'the spirit' (*go-shin*), and just before the *mikoshi* begins its festival progress, there is a ceremony to which is given the name '*kami-ire*' or the 'induction of the *kami*'; often at this ceremony, the mirror, one of the three treasures of nearly all shrines and another favourite 'spirit body', is transferred from shrine to *mikoshi*.

The present-day *mikoshi* is a small wooden ark or shrine, windowless and about four or five feet high, mounted on two thick wooden shafts which project for about fifteen feet at either end. It is so heavy that for carrying it requires all the shoulders of the young stalwarts among the shrine's parishioners that can manage to squeeze themselves a space under the shafts. But this is a later embellishment of the original form which seems to have been merely a single branch of *sakaki* mounted on a simple dais. Anciently, the people of Ishikawa Prefecture used the double term *sakaki-mikoshi*, with *sakaki* as a sort of descriptive adjective, and there are instances in early literature of the use of *o-sakaki* to signify *mikoshi*. (*O*, as the grammarians say, is an honorific prefix: you use it of others, never of yourself; you apply it more or less indiscriminately where the *kami* are involved; and you may apply it as a piece of race discrimination— *o-sake* of our own distinctive Japanese rice wine, but never *o-biru*, an inferior foreign product, *o-cha* of home-produced green tea, but never *o-kōcha*, black tea, even if it is best Darjeeling.) But *sakaki* and *mikoshi* are still not entirely divorced, for a branch of the former, carried by the chief priest of the shrine, often precedes the latter in the opening moments, if no more, of its procession. Nor was it inappropriate that the *sakaki*—the 'flourishing tree' if our derivation be correct—be used as one of the means of expelling the decay of the epidemic, the withering of the drought and the rest of the summer calamities.

The spear of the first celebration of the Gion ceremony is the tall tower, surmounted by its spear, of the float today. The spear wards off the enemy; it has the awesome property of being able to take the life from a man. It is, therefore, like the sword, good *kami* potential, and was readily regarded as a 'spirit body', the concrete object to which the spirit of a *kami* descends for a time. If the epidemic was nationwide, then the sixty-six spears would both ward off and aid in expelling the calamity from the equivalent number of administrative districts; they would at the same time attract and embody an assembly, appropriately numbered, of benevolent *kami*. Again, the spear may well have acted as a marker for the descending *kami*. Tree trunks or branches of the *sakaki* were used for this purpose, and there is still occasional observance of the practice whereby a 'mountain marker' was built to ensure the *kami*'s navigational accuracy. A mound of soil planted with a few branches was both a distinctive landmark and again a simulation of a wooded hill or mountain, the expected point of the *kami*'s arrival according to the most widely-held belief. Now, the tall floats of the Gion procession today, as well as being called simply *hoko*, spears, are also popularly described as *yamaboko*—mountain spears. They are then not only guardian personifications of the *kami*, but in addition act as marker mounds, pathfinders for the alighting *kami*. In either aspect, they should not be handled or approached by any contaminated person. Women, in virtue of their liability to the 'red' pollution, have long been barred from entering or climbing the floats—a prohibition which the American authorities waived, only to find that their relaxation met with subsequent Japanese disregard after it was linked with and judged responsible for the collapse of more than one of the floats in the course of the procession.

It is not only in July that the Gion Shrine is the focus of Kyōto's activity. Soon after dark on New Year's Eve, hordes of Kyōto's inhabitants, together with some even from as far away as Ōsaka and Kōbe, converge on the shrine and the crackling braziers and pine torches that stand in its compound. The braziers have been lit by a sacred flame and they in turn serve to kindle a length of straw rope, like the Yorkshire boy's tarband on Plot Night. The visitor to the shrine twirls his rope to keep it alight as he makes his way home, then he lights the first fire of the New Year from it: this fire and the food he cooks with it will assure his good health through the year to come. Again straw appears as the purifier, as in the case of the bundle placed in the confinement room to absorb the filth of the 'red' pollution; again the *kami* of the Gion Shrine as the guardian of health; and again the precise halving of the year—for the initial purification rite preparatory to the Gion Festival falls on the last day of the sixth month. It is a far cry from the damp steamy days at the close of Kyōto's summer rains to the biting wind which sweeps down the Kamo basin from the snow-covered hills to the north-east and the crisp air of New Year's Eve; but, whatever the season and its ailments, *Gion San* will keep you well.

Guiding the returning spirits

Five

BON

'I was disgusted with all this new-fangled hand clapping and waving: it's not at all like the real thing. And everyone has his own private version of it,' said the old man. He was seventy-two, well-built and compact, and his teeth flashed white as he smiled ironically at the modern interpretations.

The night before, we had gone to the 'Lake of the Wild Iris', a vast amusement park near Nara, Japan's first permanent capital and the cradle of her culture. To the huge natural amphitheatre in the centre of the park thronged many of the people of the district of Yamato, of which Nara is the prefectural city. Some came to watch, others to dance, for this was the last of a three-day contest to pick the best team of town or village dancers in the district. Although the programme was built round the Bon Dance, it was nevertheless a motley farrago with three main divisions: post-war Japanese dances came first; then, something billed as 'folk-dances'—we had gone expecting the gems of this tradition-loving district but we found ourselves watching instead something which, from the dancers' steps as well as from the music, might well have been a cross between a square dance and a Gay Gordons! Then, in third place, came a series of local traditional dances, all of which can be traced back in some way to the Bon Dance of Shiga Prefecture, on the shores of Lake Biwa to the north, but which soon felt the influence of their new setting in the villages of Yamato for each locality has its distinctive variations in the matter of the steps of the dance and each has added to the words of the accompanying song a local introduction and original lyrics detailing its own beauty spots.

The drum, the sole accompanying instrument for this Bon Dance, began to beat for the last of the teams. The drummer knelt on one knee, his drum placed, hide facing sideways, on a three foot high stand; bringing the sticks up from behind his shoulder, he played alternate booms on the hide and staccato taps on the wooden frame. Thirty men and women danced to his beat as it echoed round the amphitheatre. They wore the light cotton *kimono* of the summer, blue pattern on a white ground, and only white cotton ankle socks to protect their feet from the gravel floor of the amphitheatre. We were struck by the singularity of the gestures and the foot-motions of this party, from Shinjō village, a largish community down to the south of the prefecture, nestling under the foothills which lead to the high and rugged range enclosing Yamato's southern limits. There was an air of difference about Shinjō's dance; even as you looked at the teenage members of this group, there was somehow an age about their steps which set this item apart from the rest we had seen. So, at the end of the evening, when the floodlights were darkened and the tired, whimpering children in the audience had been whisked off home, we went down to the stage and spoke to Shinjō's headman.

'Yes,' he agreed, 'it is different, isn't it? And there's quite a tale to it. Come along to the village one day and we'll tell you all about it.'

We went—the very next afternoon. The headman met us at the point where the narrow village lane led off from the dusty main road and took us up to his office. The girl who had led the team the night before sat primly, in blouse and skirt now, behind a typewriter. But, in the large Japanese-style room upstairs with its floor of bamboo matting, were the old couple whom we had noticed dancing with the team.

'Mr Saika,' said the headman, introducing us to the man and ignoring the old lady.

'I was disgusted. Yes. We were fed up,' repeated old Saika San. (Even his name is rare.) As he spoke, he half

turned and inclined his head to show that 'we' included the
gentle grandmother, ten years his junior. They used words
which led us to take her for his wife and it was not until we
asked for names and addresses, so that we might send presents
after we had got back home, that we discovered they were no
more than near neighbours.

'There was far too much *garyū* about our dance, too much
individualist innovation. I couldn't stand the brittleness and
the slopping about of the modern ways. Your whole body
should be soft and pliable, shoulders and hips especially.
Never show the soles of your feet; you should walk the steps,
not slide your feet over the floor as they all do nowadays.'

Here was the definition of the difference that had attracted
us the night before.

But Saika had more to say.

'So two years ago I decided we'd try to revive the style
we used when I was a boy. I'm over seventy now and I can't
have been more than sixteen or seventeen when two men
came and stayed in the village for ten days. They came from
way up to the north-east, from a village on the shores of
Lake Biwa.'

The old man couldn't remember whether these two were
invited or not. Nara was, and still is, famous for its medicines;
it might well have happened that some medicine pedlar
from Shinjō, struck by the difference of the lakeside dances,
invited some of his clients back home to spread the knowledge of the strange movements.

'These two were both of them wonderful dancers and I
remember very clearly how they lined us all up and taught us
their way of doing things. Soon we adopted their style for our
own village dance; but it wasn't very long before we slipped
back into our old ways and this imported style was forgotten.
There's only one other person left alive now who remembers
them—but he's stone deaf and can't move an inch without
a stick in each hand. So he wasn't much help to me.'

I asked if this old style was difficult.

'Mm. She found it very difficult to get the necessary
pliancy and suppleness.'

'She' was a woman of about thirty, a *natori* (a pupil of sufficient merit to take the title of her school) of a name famous in Japan's theatre, who had also been fascinated by the distinctiveness of Shinjō's dance. She had joined in rehearsals but the old man was surprised—and yet secretly pleased—at her inability to capture this strange pliancy. And, sure enough, when they gave a demonstration, it was very easy to distinguish the odd one out.

By this time, the news of our arrival had spread. The typist from downstairs had changed back into her white and blue *kimono* of the previous night and was ready to lead the team; the drummer was warming up and the singer, in a shrill and almost screaming voice, launched into his verses, telling of the village's cherry blossoms and red maple leaves, the legends of the mountain towering to the south. Then Saika took the old lady to the centre of the bamboo-matted floor and we saw a repeat performance of those supple and rippling hand and leg movements.

Saika's restoration gained first prize for the village in competition with the whole province. Perhaps, on that account, it may stay.

'Gion ends, then Bon begins,' is a common saying in Japan. Gion's festival, with its main processions in the middle of July, and Bon with its principal rituals celebrated in the central days of August—around the full moon of the seventh month by the old lunar calendar—both fall in the farmer's slack season, when the rice has been planted out in the paddies and requires comparatively little care. So he can give these festivals a fair amount of undivided attention; and in that they coincide with the height of the summer heat, he can—and often does—indulge in some degree of forget-the-heat-frolicking on both occasions.

The usual accounts of the series of ceremonies known as Bon derive them almost completely, if not entirely so, from the Asiatic mainland. The term Bon is explained as a shortened form of the Sanscrit *Ullambana* (*Ullam*—the topsy-turvy suspension of a body, and *bana*—a tray on which food is served) and the rituals, a feast of All Souls, first celebrated in China in AD 538, and in Japan on the 15th of the seventh month (the night of the full moon) of AD 606, are said to have originated in an episode in the life of Mokuren, a disciple of the Buddha.

According to Buddhist tradition, Mokuren, perplexed at the knowledge that his mother's ravenous ghost was unable to take food, which she saw turned into fire in front of her, sought the advice of the Buddha on this dilemma. Mokuren was told to offer food and drink on the night of the 15th of the seventh month; these offerings, if properly prepared, would procure relief for parents and ancestors seven generations back, and would, further, if presented to parents still living, assure long life.

However, there are not a few points in both the historical and the present-day celebration of the Bon festival where this usual interpretation in terms of the direct import from China does far from full justice to the Japanese facts. These amply repay further and closer investigation.

The first point to notice in this connection is the very intimate relationship between Bon and Tanabata, which occurs on the seventh day of the seventh month, apparently one of the Chinese-style reduplications of identical month and day, and here, in particular, the mystic seven of China. Tanabata could well be, and is in fact often, interpreted as an import direct from China, practically unmodified during the long period of its celebration in Japan. So the bamboo decorations, with good-luck charms attached, which are put up in or before each house on this night are in honour of the two stars, the Herdsman and the Weaving Girl, lovers from of old, fated by the diverging paths of their courses to meet each other on this night alone in the whole year. Tanabata, then, is purely a star festival, based on an age-old romance of the heavens, beloved and typical of the Chinese. A certain amount of evidence bears witness to this relationship with the Chinese ceremony; one explanation of the term Tanabata, for instance, sees it as a combination of *hata*, the loom of the women who weave holy silk kneeling before the altar (*tana*) set up in honour of the spirits and ancestors who visit this world of mortals on the occasion of an important and critical juncture of seasons—in this instance, summer and autumn. Again, in court circles at least, the festival in its form as an import from China and as derived from the stellar romance, seems to have had special if not exclusive significance for the weaving girls of the capital. A document on ritual of the early tenth century, in stressing this fact, says that the celebration was in the hands of the Minister of Looms, a comparatively minor official. This gives some indication of the insignificant weight with which this aspect of the Tanabata festival was regarded, for a ceremony of greater import would have been allocated to the Bureau of Rites. In fact, in court environs at the time, the highlight of the seventh month was the Grand Sumō Tournament, a wrestling meeting which took place on the twenty-fifth.

However, there are certain practices that go to make up the Tanabata festival that cannot be explained along the lines of the Chinese stellar festival. In the first place, especially in the area about Kyōto, Tanabata is given the name *Bon Hajime* (Bon Beginning); on this day begins the work of tidying and refurbishing tombs, of cleaning wells, of washing hair and purging the body of all surface pollution, and of preparing the route from mountain to home on which the spirits returning for Bon are expected to travel. In this light Tanabata is clearly the day which marks the beginning of all Bon preparations, the start of a pre-*matsuri* period of fasting and purification, in purpose not unlike the *komori*. This is the significance of 'Seventh Day Bon', another term for Tanabata.

The Bon festival is, in essence, of the standard type of *matsuri*—the welcoming, joint entertainment and then the escorted departure of a returning spirit—so that all must be made ready and clean for the presence of the honoured guest. Thus, consequent on the notion that on the seventh the preparation for the advent of the ancestral spirits begins, there came about the belief that on the same day, the spirits set out on their long journey home from the far beyond—the location and features of which have been and are still only very vaguely conceived. For whereas the most general belief is that the souls of the ancestors return home from the mountains nearby—or at least, that this is the last stage of a longer journey—in many seaside villages on the shores of the Kii peninsula, and in Mie, the soul abode is thought of as far across the seas; and on the night of the sixth, or early in the morning of the seventh of the seventh month, small boats of reeds, provisioned with purified rice, beans and vegetables are launched on the sea to drift of their own to the land of the spirits and furnish the means of their return.

Nor does Tanabata merely mark the beginning of Bon preparations; in a few particulars, Bon and Tanabata practice is identical. One such instance is the preparation at Tanabata of grasses or straw, in the shape of miniature horses, as decorations to be set up at the house door or gate. There is here a close parallel with the straw horses of Bon—for the ancestors to mount and ride home—as there is also in the method of disposal of these horses; in both festivals, they are often floated down river, or across the sea.

There is another significant relationship between Tanabata and Bon, for the night on which Tanabata is celebrated is not only that of the meeting of the Weaving Girl and the Herdsman, but also that of the half-moon of Bon's full moon. There are some localities where Bon preparations start as early as on the first day of the seventh month and the final rituals are not completed until the thirtieth day—occupying the whole of the lunar month; if that was the original scope of the festival in certain areas—and everything points to a gradual scaling down in scope and length in the case of a good many celebrations of this nature—and if the night of the full moon marked the climax of the festival, it would not be unnatural if the half-moon were regarded as the mark for the commencement of the last stage of preparation and pre-festival purification.

In its most general form—though there is a considerable variety in the details of its celebration—Bon begins with the lighting of torches or fires both in front of the house and before the tomb on the thirteenth day of the seventh month; that such flames are intended to act as markers for the returning ancestral spirits, as well as to purify the premises in readiness for and during the interval of the presence of the spirits is clear from the importance placed on them in the case of 'New' or 'Fresh Bon' households—families in which there has been a death since the last celebration of Bon, and where, consequently, there will be a spirit making the journey home for the very first time. In such cases, in many areas, it is customary to mark both the route and the house with specially prominent fires—pine torches tied to the top of long bamboo poles—to light newly prepared lanterns in the room set apart for the spirits and to mark the entrance to the house with, literally, 108 torches. Here, there is a parallel with New Year practice, for it is with the hundred and eighth toll of the bell at midnight on the last day of the old year that the various sins and defilements of the old are purged and all is made clean and pure for the new.

Also on the thirteenth, clear water, freshly drawn from the well, is placed before the door, where the returning spirits may bathe their feet and refresh themselves after their tiring journey. And not a few households will tell you that, on the following morning, this water bears unmistakable traces of mud or soil. The principal remaining task of the preparations of the thirteenth is the decoration and the furnishing of the *Bondana*, the shelf for offerings, sometimes as large as three or four feet long and one foot or more wide. Again, in the case of 'New Bon' households, it is important that extra care and concern be evinced by an early state of preparedness; so, in many cases, the Bon shelves are made ready even on the first day of the month, or, more regularly, by the seventh, Tanabata day. The Bon shelf, where it is imagined in many instances that the spirit resides for the period of its sojourn, as well as holding the offerings of food and drink, is decorated with Bon flowers, picked in the mountains early on the morning of either the eleventh or the thirteenth. There is considerable local variation in the types of flower used, though the Chinese bellflower, a variety of patrinia and loosestrife appear most commonly. The ancestral spirits of the household are thus amply provided for. But should there be any 'hungry souls' returning with the rest— 'hungry' in that the dead with no living descendants have none to care for and make offerings to them—to appease them, a separate 'hungry soul shelf' is often placed near the true Bon shelf, or at the front of the house.

With all preparations completed, the returning spirits are met—usually in the hills, sometimes at the water's edge in the case of a seaside community—and are led fondly back to the house. The guide will often go to the extent of an elaborate series of make-believe gestures; he will carefully point the path, or arch his back, clasp his hands behind him and make as if he were carrying an aged parent on his shoulders—for in mountain areas where any form of wheel communication is difficult, there is an age-old tradition that the old, and grandmother in particular, are transported in this fashion.

The fourteenth and fifteenth are rest days; then, on the evening of the fifteenth or in the early morning of the six- teenth, the sending-off ceremonies begin. There is little evidence that the ancestors are thought of as returning to the grave. The most widely observed method of escorting them from their homes points to the conception that they set out on a long sea journey; provisions for this, the offerings on the Bon shelf, are wrapped in leaves and loaded into small straw boats and these, with their candle flames winking forlornly as they grow more distant, are floated off down river or into the offing. In some instances the straw horses that were made for Tanabata serve as mounts for the return- ing spirits and these too are launched in the water. Special attention is given sometimes to the offerings for the 'hungry' spirits, only these being floated away from the village con- fines; the motive is no doubt to ensure that such not very welcome guests be despatched as soon as may appear seemly —after all, they did gate-crash and their continued presence, by their very hungry nature and their resultant capacity for evil, constitutes a potential source of calamity. The spirit

*Weather forecasting at Little New Year by bamboo
tubes and a pan of rice gruel*

boats have their name and destination, written sometimes on leaves festooning the straw bows—'The Boat for the West' (the Heaven in the West of Amidism) or 'The Good Ship Paradise' and so on.

The true function of the Bon Dance is to comfort and exhilarate the spirits—especially the havoc-wreaking 'hungry ones—either just prior to or at the time of their departure. It is thus most properly performed on the evening of the fifteenth, the last night of the spirits' visit—and the night of the full moon. Most often, the dancers congregate in the village square, though in the case of seashore and riverside communities, they sometimes enter the water as the spirit boats depart. In rare instances, the neighbourhood of the ancestors' tombs is the site of the dance. Once again, 'New Bon' households are singled out for special treatment; the dancers may break the circle and go the rounds of the community, pausing a little before each 'New Bon' house; or again, it is not uncommon for the dancers to form their ring round the Bon shelves and the lanterns brought from such recently bereaved families and placed in some open spot in the centre of the village. There is now practically no sex segregation of the dancers, though formerly there did occur instances of distinct male and female teams, or of men wearing women's, and women wearing men's clothing. The steps and gestures of the dance are comparatively simple, the accompaniment is usually restricted to the drum as in Shinjō village (though flutes and gongs are included in some instances), and the words of the song—the singer often bellowing down from the top of a precarious-looking tower in the centre of the ring of dancers—are in the form of a four-line stanza, with a rhythm of 7.7.7.5. syllables, in contrast to the usual alternation of five- and seven-syllable lines in the literary verse of Japan.

There is a variety of names other than Bon Dance given to this final ceremony of Bon; it includes Dance of Offerings, Spirit Dance, Dance of the Tombs, Dance of the Eighth Month (which clearly derives from a date subsequent to the calendrical reforms) and, significantly, Dance of the Fruitful Year.

It will be clear from this account of the main features of the Bon festival that there is a deal more to it than can be adequately explained in terms of a simple and straightforward incorporation of a Chinese Buddhist memorial ceremony. First, there are hints that Bon is in some aspects a preparation for the harvest, a ritual designed to ensure that the crops yield well. Thus, one name for the Bon Dance is, as has just been noted, Dance of the Fruitful Year. The purpose of the ritual dance in Japan is not only to give thanks or to celebrate a good that is already provided; it can also act as an insurance, as a magic inducer of a future blessing. Again, if performed on its proper occasion, the evening of the fifteenth, it marks the night of the full moon of the seventh month, the first moon of autumn, the season of the harvest; for Chinese practice, soon adopted with Chinese writing in Japan, was to count the start of the year as the beginning of spring, the seventh month as the first autumn month and so on.

In some cases, in one of the closing ceremonies of the series of Bon rituals, tinder materials are placed at the top of a high pole; the villagers gather round this pole, with pine torches in their hands, lit from a sacred flame blessed at their parish shrine, and hurl these torches up towards the straw-waste tinder, in an attempt to set fire to it. Here, for one thing, there is the element of contest at the crisis time of the important juncture of the seasons which we have noticed before at the New Year, and to which we must return later; this practice is also connected closely with the harvest: in Kyūshū for instance, the direction in which this pole falls, after it has caught fire and burnt down, constitutes a principal basis for divination on the question whether the year's crops will be fruitful or otherwise. In some areas, and especially around the base of Mount Fuji, the torch tossing ceremony is often held instead on the first of the month (another instance of the change in emphasis from full to new moon time) or on the seventh, Tanabata night.

Again, from the fact that the decorations of the Bon shelves often include the first fruits of vegetable crops, the new rice, and of winter-cherry, it is evident that at the onset of Bon, the farmer's thoughts begin to turn to his maturing harvests; and the connection between Bon and harvest is strengthened further by the use of the bamboo branches of the Tanabata decorations as scarecrows in paddies and other fields where the several crops are ripening. There is a similar connection between the harvest and the Midsummer Eve fires of Europe; the fires are likewise both divinatory—the corn will grow as high as the flames leap—and protective—the charred wood was taken from the embers and, stuck in the fields on the night of the festival, was left there until the harvest had been brought in safely. And the special attention paid to 'New Bon' households throughout the festival, particularly the fact that the Bon Dance, inviting and inducing a good harvest, takes place sometimes with 'New Bon' household offerings as its focal point, may be paralleled by the primacy given to newly weds in the case of Midsummer Eve Fires; in some instances the fires were built and other important functions fulfilled by men or couples married since the previous celebration of the midsummer festival.

Not only is Bon, by the old lunar reckoning, the signal for the opening of the autumn; with the New Year (taking the day of the full moon as the starting point, the modern 'Little New Year') it forms a much more important dividing point of the year. The Japanese terms for the two markers are, for New Year, the 'First Beginning', and for Bon, the 'Middle Beginning'. From this arises the term the 'Year-adding of Bon', used occasionally in the case of households where there has been no death in the period since the last Bon festival; and it is clearly, as at New Year, a matter for congratulation that this momentous stage in the year's course has been reached safely from the greeting on the morning of the thirteenth—'The compliments of the season to you, on the occasion of your splendid Bon'.

With Bon the marker of the start of a new half year, as well as in the presence of not only ancestral but 'hungry' and potentially evil spirits, it is even more important that ceremonies to perfect ritual purification be carefully executed. This is part of the purpose of the several fire and water ceremonies in the Tanabata and Bon series, for these are the two most potent purgers known to Japanese ritual practice. A well-marked change of season is often the time chosen for a periodic expulsion of evils and impurities, and the spirit boats of Bon in Japan, sometimes laden, be it noted, with offerings made to the 'hungry' spirits only, are common to many of the lands of the Pacific area. Anciently, for example, in Perak, there was a wide-ranging round-up of evil spirits every seven years, or once in a Rajah's reign; they were bundled on to large bamboo rafts and allowed to drift down the Perak River and out to sea. The evil spirit ship of the Babar Islands is fitted up with two bowls, one filled with ashes from every kitchen in the community desiring a purging of the pollution and the other containing the spittle of every sick man. It is by no means the urging of altruistic motives that spurs the celebrator of Bon in Japan to offer food and service to the 'hungry' spirit who lacks descendants; for though the family and even the community spirit is exceptionally strong, especially on the occasion of ceremonies of this nature, it would not lead to actions the scope of which went beyond the limits of the maxim 'look after your own', 'your own' applying to the members of the immediate family, or in the wider context, of the whole community. The 'hungry' ghost, however, has no place in the parish registers; it is as an object of dread at a critical juncture in the year, when the seeds of disaster may be sown, and not as a recipient of pity, that he is treated generously and escorted ceremoniously but safely far off the premises.

But Bon is not given over entirely to lamentation and skulking dread. Like the New Year, it is a matter for felicitation that you have arrived at this milestone in the year without calamity, and it is in this respect that the New Year and Bon ceremonies show the greatest similarities. There are widespread instances, where the parents are both still living, of children giving them congratulatory presents of fish on the thirteenth or fourteenth, and there is evidence that this practice existed in the mid-fifteenth century, with the gift of *sake* and fish on the eleventh day of the month.

This congratulation of the living is explained as a straight-forward counterpart of the service of the spirits of the dead, and it is described in Japanese by terms such as 'The Bon of the Living Man' or 'Souls of the Living', the terms being identical with those used of worship of the spirits at New Year. Buddhist observance would eschew not only the slaughter of all living things at the time of Bon, but also the eating of meat or fish. The type of fish most commonly used for this congratulatory present is a kind of mackerel, which, in the countryside around Tokyo, sons will go out to catch specially for the occasion, and which wives in various areas will take home to the village of their birth. Here again, there is the magic of the play on identically sounding words, and the use of the magic, as so often, as a harvest charm, or as a means of procuring a badly desired end; for the name for this type of mackerel, pronounced *saba*, is homonymous with a word meaning 'productive' or 'birth food'. Bon is also the season for gifts other than those of children to living parents; relationships between craftsman and apprentice, master and servant, friend and friend and so on are honoured at this time, and again this practice, paralleled by an identical one at New Year, is often described by the same word *seibo*—'year-end present', or by the term meaning 'The Middle Beginning' of the year.

There are other close similarities and relationships between these two ceremonies that divide the year so neatly. In some instances, offerings left over or ceremonial implements deliberately saved from the one are put to use in the celebration of the other six months later; thus, a handful of chestnut chopsticks first used at Bon is offered to the ancestors along with the New Year rice. The mountain flower-gathering expeditions on the eleventh day to furnish Bon decorations find an exact counterpart in the journeys to the hills on the eleventh day of the New Year, journeys made 'to meet the young wood', to gather freshly-cut branches that will constitute the ceremonial ornaments of the 'Little New Year' ritual of the fifteenth day. In each case it is believed, in some quarters at least, that the ancestral spirits return to their homes together with these decorative flowers and branches.

The ceremonies of each of these half-year festivals often include some with an element of contest about them, the outcome of the contest furnishing a basis for divination about

The divinatory tug of war at Bon

the most vital event—the weather prospects for rice planting, the amount of the harvest, whether from the sea or from the paddy—of the subsequent period. If such contests are staged in the presence of the returning spirits, their outcome can be interpreted as an indication of the spirits' intentions and wishes. The torch-hurling ceremony already noticed had something of the spirit of the contest about it, but in the tug of war, and the constitution of the rival teams, this element of divinatory strife at critical junctures is much more apparent. The tug of war, generally a New Year ceremony in the eastern half of Japan and part of the Bon festival in the west—though this is a very broad distinction admitting of a fair number of exceptions—is often staged only after a series of ceremonies designed to drive off all evil spirits whose presence might endanger and falsify the outcome. The contest usually takes place on the road that serves the village; the rope sometimes is made in the shape of a huge serpent. The opposing teams are picked from different sections of a community, the divisions marking either occupational or geographical units. Thus they may represent the fishing and the farming sections of the village; if fishermen win, their catch will be more prolific than the crops of the farmer: or in a purely agricultural district, the rival sides may be chosen from those who farm rice paddies and those engaged in dry cultivation. If there is a residence basis for the division of the teams, Upper and Lower for example, the result is interpreted as an indication not so much of a differing yield in the districts in question as of the possible trends in the price of rice after the harvest is in; if the Upper team wins, then prices will soar, and all, wherever their residence, will enjoy a carefree winter. In fishing or seaside settlements, the contest at the time of the division of the year often takes the form of a boat race. The most celebrated of such races—those at Nagasaki in early May, with thirty or forty rowers in a small boat, as many as seventy in a large one—as well as those of the south-western coastal district of Kyūshū are often interpreted in terms of a direct import of a simple contest from Southern China. But, particularly in the coastal districts of Okayama, in the western part of the main island, these contests also occur in the Bon season; and at the New Year, the ritual practice of the first going on board of the year and the subsequent race between fishing craft are almost universal.

Children's activities figure prominently in both festivals. Children often build small and crude huts on comparatively high ground, or away from the settled area of their village and there they will spend a day or two in a *komori* restricted only to children. They may, too, build a hearth out of doors and live completely independently of their elders for the first two days of the festival. After the *komori* has been concluded, the huts are often set fire to, the children dancing round the flames and brandishing pine torches. In Tokushima, the home of the famous Awa Odori, the most spectacular of

the Bon dances in the whole of Japan, the name given to these
fires built from the *komori* huts and lit very early on the
morning of the fourteenth is *sagichō*—the term, that is, for
the similar burning of the children's vigil huts on, usually,
the evening of the fourteenth of the New Year.

Here, once more, is the element of the use of fire in these
festivals. It may be that, as with the fires lit to send off and
escort the returning ancestors, this hut-burning is also to be
understood as a part of the ritual in honour of the guests
soon to depart. But this explanation is not wholly satisfactory
and from the fact that these vigil huts, especially in the New
Year festival, are often placed astride the confines of the
community territory, or near to important means of entry
to or exit from it, as well as in that much of the ritual
concerning the cult of the tutelary spirits of village territory
seems from the earliest times to have been given over to
children, it may well be that such fires are intended primarily
to drive off any harmful influences at the critical moment on
the eve of the first full moon of the new half-year period.

There are, then, a number of vastly differing sources that
go to make up the sum of the Bon festival. Practice varies
with locality for a variety of reasons; some areas, comparatively hostile to Buddhism throughout their development,
have maintained more of and given greater emphasis to the
indigenous or even pre-Buddhist aspects of this heterogeneous
whole. In other districts where Buddhism, and every reli-
gous faith, for that matter, has been avidly and indiscriminately incorporated, the Buddhist-influenced elements
stand out more noticeably. Yet, though there is much that is
not Buddhist-derived in the Bon festival, a good many of
such elements other than the Buddhist are in fact of a nature
very similar to the Buddhist. This may be dismissed as the
latter influencing and modulating the former, but such an
explanation would not do ample justice to the facts; both, it
seems, of the main sources of the Bon ceremony had to do
with a soul festival. The close similarity between New Year
and Bon rituals derives in many cases from their being both
in honour of returning ancestral spirits, and to mark, in the

presence of these spirits, the beginning of another important half-year season. And although it is conventional, with those who interpret Bon as an incorporation of the Chinese ceremony, to explain the term Bon as a drastic contraction of *Ullambana*, the character often employed for Bon in many old records was also used to signify an earthenware vessel to hold offerings made to ancestral spirits, or to mean 'to hold celebrations to honour' such spirits. So the very name of the festival, far from being a loan from Buddhism, 'Japped' and maltreated in the way of most such linguistic loans, may well be a relic of an old indigenous soul festival. Purification is an essential prelude to every ritual celebration in Japan; before a ceremony of such moment, self-purification and the banishment of all polluting and malicious influences becomes even more vital. So it comes about that in some aspects the Bon festival appears to be little more than a continuation of the summer rituals of the (lunar) sixth month, with their stress on water and fire, the great purifiers, and their ceremonies designed to banish all the evil spirits of disease and sickness in the steamy heat that follows the summer rains. And finally, Bon marks the threshold of the autumn, the start of concern about and efforts at least to learn about, if not at times to control, the yield of the fields.

And—to return to our point of departure—the Bon Dance may well be interpreted in part as a piece of midsummer madness the like of which occurs in many cultures other than Japan's.

> You're a fool if you dance,
> And a fool if you watch.
> You're a fool either way—
> So you may as well dance.
> (Lyric of the Awa Odori, Bon Dance of
> Tokushima, Shikoku)

Six

RAINMAKING

The rice shoots are planted out in the paddies in the middle weeks of June just after the start of the rainy season, the 'plum rains'. The sky is leaden. Drizzle falls day after day. Shoes are covered in mildew overnight and when the sun does break through, it steams up the damp from the roofs and the fields. It is an unhappy time for the townsman who uses his summer bonus, a month's salary paid in June in addition to his normal wage, to buy the odd drink with his colleagues after work and to brighten up life amidst all this drabness. But the farmer works on, for this is one of the busiest seasons of his year. He strips to the waist, goes barefoot and rolls his trousers up above his knees; as he stoops to press in a plant, the waters of his paddy reach almost to his thighs. He flings a bundle of rice shoots from the narrow pathway at the edge of the field to the workers in the water and the bright emerald flash stands out starkly against the dull background. Then, his plants once set, he prays for a little more rain; after that, for a hot, baking sun to bring on his crop and ripen the ears.

But in some years it turns out that the rainy season is not wet enough to give the rice crops their first grounding. This happened in a recent year. The rainy season brought no rain to speak of in June; July and the early part of August were abnormally dry and the last two weeks of August and the first part of September saw a series of unusually early and heavy typhoon rainstorms. According to an old piece of weather lore, typhoons should not appear before the 'two hundred and tenth day', the first of September when you start the reckoning from New Year's Day in early February according to the old lunar calendar.

That year, we visited the village of Iwashimizu on August 13th—lucky thirteen as it turned out. Iwashimizu lies just over twenty miles south of Nara and is tucked away in the broad range of hills which separates southern Yamato from the coastal plain of Ise. The village had had no rain now for more than fifty days, not even the short sharp shower that falls on a July or August evening in these parts when the year is not abnormal. The mountain streams which flow through

Rice planting

the village territory and are used for crop irrigation had been reduced to the merest trickle quite inadequate for the task. Huge cracks had begun to gape across some of the dry-cultivation fields, some of them too wide to jump even, unless you could take a run at them. So Iwashimizu's farmers had been driven in the end to the old expedient of a rain-making ritual, as had already happened on two occasions since the war, first in 1948 and again in 1955.

It was just after one o'clock as we arrived. The noon sun baked the dusty earthen road that serves the village. As you looked up beyond the houses to the hills, the ground shimmered for at this height there were few trees to shield the sun's power and no breath of wind stirred the parched grass. On the slope which rose sharply above the road stood a windowless, single-storey shack which went by the imposing name of 'Iwashimizu Community Agricultural Advisory Hall'. Inside the Hall's single room which was dark and airless, for only one of its wooden shutters had been drawn back, three old men, two of them accompanied by their wives, sat round a huge unlit *hibachi*-brazier which they used as a magnificent ash-tray. Their legs were crossed and their

Sickles, to cut the wind before it damages the house, are placed at each end of the roof ridge at the start of the typhoon season

hands rested on the lip of the brazier. One of them chain-smoked his Golden Bat cigarettes; he would light a fresh one, take two drags on it and then nick it midway, fitting the lighted half into a stained and dirty holder which crackled like a coke boiler each time he drew through it. None of the five spoke, but their sullen immobility was broken for the moment as they looked round occasionally to the further end of the hall, where, in the shadows, there flickered two candles flanking a length of smouldering rope. This rope was enclosed in an oval-shaped wicker windbreak fastened near the top of a seven-foot length of bamboo. By the side of this holy fire stood a low table with a dirty cloth and on it fruit and cake offerings, now withered and dry.

Soon, the village headman came in from his rounds to tell the story. The community comprised sixty-four households; these five were the only members too old and weak to be out on their lands doing what little they could to nurse their crops through the drought. Since the ritual was a community function, expenses were shared out equally between each household and each again had to provide one member for the duty of the vigil by the holy fire. In the daytime only these five—and sometimes not even all of them—were available for this task, but by the evening, as the able-bodied members came in from their fields and the children got back from school, the room would be full.

Four days before, continued the headman, two young men had set out from the village to catch the electric train to the foot of Mount Kōya, there to wait as the fire they were to use for their rainmaking ceremony was blessed and applied to a piece of slow-burning rope. The only consideration that had guided him in the selection of these two was that they should be the two toughest specimens available, for they must walk and jog-trot the thirty-five miles of hard going back to the village. Once they had received the fire from Mount Kōya's priests, it must be kept on the move until it reached village territory. They were ordered to take their meals by relays, biting at a ball of rice as they walked, and were to shake the fire as often and as vigorously as they could, while yet ensuring that the smouldering rope stayed alight. The word *furu* which means 'to shake' is also the word used for 'to fall' of rain. The one action should induce the other.

Once these two returned with the holy fire, the long wait and watch began. But more could be done. By going to Mount Kōya, the villagers had already invoked the assistance of the sect of Buddhism of which it is the headquarters: they had offered thanksgiving tokens to the spirit of their parish Shintō shrine in the event of the grant of rain: they might also invite their local Buddhist priest to say the sutra at the Agricultural Advisory Hall, in front of the sacred fire. So they had summoned such a priest, who came twice in the day. But in fact his temple was not the parish one and his sect, Zen, was not that usually intimately connected with rain-making practices. In both aspects, the choice appeared at first to be strange, for, if the ritual was essentially a community affair, its efficacy marred by the failure of any of the village people to take part, an outsider—and especially one with so vital a role to play—might be expected to work the same effect as a defaulting insider.

The Zen priest came at about five in the afternoon. He read his sutra for about ten minutes, kneeling in the shadows in front of the sacred fire. His pleasant monotone droned on for interminable passages, interrupted at their end by convulsive heaves as he ran out of breath and sucked in through closed teeth to fill his lungs for the next section.

As he read, the schoolchildren came in and began to chatter to each other. The gloomy atmosphere of the hall began to lift a little as the younger ones among them clattered over the boards of the floor and sang the songs they had learned in their lessons. Most of them did not realize the extent of the calamity threatening their lives—the break-up of their home, perhaps, they themselves put out to adoption with a distant relative, if one wealthy enough existed; if not, with a complete stranger seeking an heir to carry on his family name. Soon, the five old people teetered off to their homes for a meal after their vigil and their places were taken by the younger members of other families coming in from their fields as the darkness grew. In all, there were about fifteen of the villagers there as we came away. They were all tense and hopeful for on the third night of the ceremonies when they had last performed them, a good rain had fallen and had broken the drought. They were now entering on the third night of their vigil.

It was just beginning to spit with rain as I got back home to Nara. I rang up Iwashimizu's 'Community Agricultural Advisory Hall' straightaway.

'Yes. It's absolutely pouring down,' yelled the headman. You could detect the glee in his shouts, in place of the hollow deadness of the afternoon. That was all he had time to say. He had to change into his robes of office and lead his villagers in a thanksgiving prayer at their parish shrine. Then he must beat the drum to set the time for their all-night celebration dances.

Most of the features of Iwashimizu's rainmaking rituals are common to other villages in the area and a good many of them reappear all over Japan. The ceremonies are almost always community efforts with each household paying its share of any expenses incurred and providing at least one member for a labour corps to perform the duties they involve. Iwashimizu's expenses were far from light. First there was the fee to the priests of Mount Kōya for the provision and blessing of the holy fire; they charged 1,500 yen—about £1 10s od— for fire which would retain rainmaking potency for a week; if, by the end of this period, no rain had fallen, they reduced their charge for a renewal of the fire for another week to five hundred yen. In addition, there was the value of offerings vowed to the spirit of the local Shintō shrine in the event of a grant of rain (by far the most costly item), the fee to the sutra-reading priest, the price of the offerings on the table in front of the sacred fire and a host of other incidentals. All in all, the expenses for a week of rainmaking ritual came to about fifteen thousand yen and even a sixty-fourth part of this sum was in fact no insignificant item in the budget of a family faced with utter ruin if its crops were to fail. Few of the households had any members who went outside the village boundaries to work and there was no secondary industry or other means of replacing the lost income on which the community could rely. This district, for lack of any sizeable river, always feels the effect of drought earlier and more severely than most areas in Japan; so while the upland small-holding farmers here were sullenly pondering how they could manage to live through the winter, the larger scale and well-to-do plainsmen farmers up to the north-east of Tokyo were buying their television sets by the hordes in anticipation of bumper crops in the autumn. The nearest the Iwashimizu householder got to television was seeing the advertisements in the radio and electric gadgets shop in Sakurai, his market town down in the plains.

It is easy to understand why such stress is placed on community solidarity. In a matter such as a drought or a general crop blight which affects the whole population so gravely, the more universal the response, the more insistent become the prayers and the greater the effect of the rituals. The village deity is the guardian spirit of everyone living within his boundaries; failure by any party to participate in any joint entreaty might induce him to conclude that circumstances, after all, are not so drastic as to call for his all-out assistance.

Even in these days of benevolent central control and amidst the shoots of a welfare state shrub, penalties in case of default are easily applied. In the great majority of rural areas it is still the rule that all able-bodied males become firemen in the event of a conflagration within the boundaries of their community or, dressed in oilskins and straw rain-clothing, turn out as a typhoon wind blows and the rains it brings flood down. Amidst the general disorder it would be easy to neglect the property or the safety of any householder who bilked his community dues or whose sense of oneness with the rest was not sufficiently developed or practised. The remainder of the community divides the labour in a home where death occurs; one member from each household goes to the bereaved home, and while the men prepare the funeral paraphernalia and dig the grave, the women move in on the kitchen and perform all the additional tasks that such calamity brings. The bereaved family is left free of all tasks, its only duty to receive and to entertain condoling visitors. But the household that neglects its community duties commands no such sympathetic aid in its time of distress. Again, in districts where smallholdings are the rule, it is not uncommon for expensive agricultural machinery, indispensable to the maintenance of present-day high crop standards, to be the property of the community as a whole. Removal from the roster of those eligible to use it would be disastrous. With such powerful sanctions readily applicable, instances of default are rare indeed.

The vigil before Iwashimizu's holy fire is another feature common to rainmaking ceremonial in Japan. The villagers had contracted to wait and watch for a week and seemed not unprepared to continue for a further seven days if that proved necessary. By modern standards this was painstaking for, whereas ancient usage was to maintain the vigil for a whole month, present-day habit cuts the period to three or four days, with a week something of an exception. In holding the vigil in the Agricultural Hall, Iwashimizu acted contrary to normal practice which is to gather for such purposes in some sacred building, the parish shrine or, if one exists, the hall of the Buddhist temple. In such cases, the motive of the action is to be with, to live alongside the deity and by your constant proximity to him and to his building, to draw his attention to the act you are performing within his sacred precincts. But again there has been a fall in standards, for where the essence of the ritual demands the presence of representatives of the entire community, some villages today rarely muster more than two or three members for such a vigil and in some cases it is even agreed that a shrine official takes over such duties in return for a fee. Again, with its five old people in the daytime and a good dozen in the early evening, Iwashimizu's showing was fairly good.

Another form that rainmaking ritual may take is the 'hundred-fold' or the 'thousand-fold lustration'. Residents of a village where rain is urgently needed will proceed to the bed of a river running through their territory, perform a ritual purification there, offer a prayer and then, picking up small stones from the river bed, go with them to the parish shrine. Again the purpose is to indicate the urgency of the petition by means of the large numbers of those who make the prayer or the frequency with which their prayers are repeated. If a member of each household participates, and if he collects ten pebbles in the course of each lustration, the pile will soon be high in front of the parish deity's shrine. Of course the number in the term 'thousand-fold lustration' is not to be taken literally—'ten-thousand-fold' even occurs—it is merely a stylization. If one lustration counts for ten, one pebble for ten, the thousand mark can soon be reached. Again, as with the matter of the representation of the entire community at a ritual vigil, the feeling is that the more compelling the total number of the petitioners, the more persistent and earnest their entreaties, the easier it is to enforce the compliance of any tutelary deity, however obdurate he may be.

Where corporate action between communities similarly affected by drought is practicable, it is frequently taken, on the principle that two villages can demand more attention to their pleas than one. On the night of the seventh of August, two days before Iwashimizu sent its two young stalwarts to receive sacred fire from Mount Kōya's priests, bonfires burned at the peak of many of the orange grove hills of Wakayama Prefecture to the south. The district is one of the most famous of Japan's orange producing areas and the beacons had been built by the joint effort of over thirty communities which cultivated the groves on the thousand-foot slopes and were threatened with hard living in the year to come if their fruit were to be dried up. Just after dusk, a procession, consisting of one member from each household in all of the thirty villages, began to wind its way to the summit of the steep groves and there, by the light of lanterns and to the accompaniment of gongs and bells, the sutra was read for an hour. Then a sacred flame, brought earlier in the day from Mount Kōya, was applied to the several mounds of twigs and branches piled at the summit of the hills. If beacons as conspicuous as these did not attract due attention, then nothing would.

That night three thousand local farmers and growers tended the fire, chanted and lent their efforts to the rituals. For statistical purposes, their efforts would be calculated individually: there were three thousand prayers, three thousand pilgrimages, three thousand chantings of the words of the rainmaking incantation. So if these representatives

merely repeated ten times the simple formula of the invocation—'Grant us rain, spirit of our lands'—and if the individual were reckoned as counting for ten men, a very impressive total of three hundred thousand invocations could be
chalked up.

But these orange growers did not pin all their hopes
blindly on the trusted methods of their ancestors. They
showed a nice sense of the ability—so common in Japan but
not often so appropriately indulged—to blend the faiths of
the past with the science of their day, for during the previous
twelve hours most of them had been working frantically to
make ready for the operation of a pipe-line pump which was
to move water from the valley streams up to the parched and
barren hills. (The Japanese are ever ready to adapt old
adages to modern contexts. There is a hoary saying that,
after a great war, will occur heavy rains. In the course of a
long drought in June and July of 1934, the farmers of
Kyūshū approached the military authorities stationed in their
district with a request for an artillery bombardment which
would simulate the 'great war'. The authorities complied;
on July 8th, the Kumamoto Division let off 250 rounds of
medium field gun fire and further to the north the Kurume
Division fired a similar number of field guns and 300 rounds
from mountain artillery. The latter seems to have been the
more effective, for a violent evening storm which hit north
Kyūshū on July 9th took a day longer to reach the Kumamoto
district.)

Fire plays a prominent part in many rainmaking rituals.
Just as the 'shaking' (*furu*) of the sacred fire by Iwashimizu's
flame-carriers would induce the consonant 'fall' of rain
(*furu*), so water will be engendered to extinguish flames as
prominent as those of the beacons on the summit of Wakayama's orange groves. But there is further point in this
frequent use of fire. For by the theory of the Five Elements,
originally Chinese but introduced to Japan early in her
history, any event, whether of this earth or of the skies, may
be explained as the product of the interplay of the principles
of wood, earth, fire, metal and water. One of the several

orders in which the five were enumerated in early China was according to their destructive potentiality; thus, fire destroys wood, water destroys fire and so on. So you brandish your fire as ostentatiously as you can, with the desire that this display will be marked and will be followed by the natural fall of rain to restore the due balance upset by the excesses of your fire.

Certain Shintō and Buddhist foundations have gained fame as centres whose sacred fire is especially effective in the production of rain. In the area surrounding Mount Kōya this mountain, with the headquarters building of the Shingon—'True Word'—Sect of Buddhism sprawling over twenty-five square miles of its summit, takes a significant role in rainmaking ceremonies. Many villages send runners to receive the sacred fire at the hands of its priests from a flame never allowed to go out. Iwashimizu was the twelfth community in the area to have made use of Kōya's fire during the drought period of early August. The Shingon Sect has had for centuries a particularly intimate connection with rain ceremonies. Saint Kōbō, the founder of the Sect and the builder of Mount Kōya's monasteries, is the rainmaker *par excellence* of Japanese tradition and is remembered in the lore of villages as far apart as the north-east tip of the mainland and Shikoku and Kyūshū, the southern islands of the chain, for his deeds connected with water and related to a number of aspects of the farmer's year. In the guise of a mendicant priest, leaning heavily on his staff, he would hobble into a village and ask for water to drink. Where he was treated with kindness, he would plant his staff in the ground and from the spot would gush forth a well of clear and sweet water which has never failed to this day: but where his request was refused or was grudgingly met, a fresh, bubbling stream would turn forthwith into a muddy torrent which could never again be used for drinking water. It is widely believed that rice planting is best started on the day of the dog; farmers will cite the legend that when Saint Kōbō returned from China, carrying in his sleeve three precious grains of a high-quality rice, he was startled by the

bark of a dog and as his hands moved in self-protection, the
grains slipped from his clothing; but the rice grew where it
had fallen and matured to yield a harvest the excellence and
the quantity of which had never been known.

Saint Kōbō is connected intimately with the traditional
history of Shinsenen, Garden of the Spirit Stream, which lies
in the north-west corner of the old central square of Kyōto.
Shinsenen's grounds were originally much more grand than
they are today, for its parklands, rebuilt and restored several
times during the fourteenth and fifteenth centuries, were
finally taken away and added to the lands of the Second
Street Castle, built in 1597 to the north of the Garden.
Because of its close link with Saint Kōbō, the Garden of the
Spirit Stream became famous in both court and less exalted
circles as possessing an unusual facility both for bringing rain
and, in the event of previous deluges, for stopping excessive
falls. Today, Shinsenen is perhaps unique in that it has a
certain class of parishioners who are registered on its books
for rainmaking purposes only, but who for all other matters
are attached to their own local shrines. These rain-prayer
parishioners live some distance from the Garden, beyond the
hills to the north-east of Kyōto, by the shores of Lake Biwa
and, further north, in the Tamba area. Just as the villagers of
Iwashimizu took turns in keeping vigil at their Agricultural
Advisory Hall, the rain-prayer parishioners of Shinsenen used
to send some of their number to the Garden's shrine to
observe the ritual for five or seven days: but nowadays
standards have slackened and they come only on the first,
fourth and seventh days of a seven-day vigil. Sometimes they
will not even put themselves to this discomfort; a telephone
call to the head priest is sufficient—he is then left to his own
devices to take what measures he feels will break the
drought. A man now in his mid-forties, this officiant will tell
you eagerly and earnestly of his first experience: a schoolboy
of sixteen at home for the summer holidays, he was begged by
a group of village representatives to take measures which
would stop a long continued rainy spell; his father, chief
priest at the time, was travelling in a district too remote to

allow of a return early enough to benefit the villagers so the boy himself made the attempt and none seems to have been more astounded than he at his immediate success. With a self-satisfied smile, he will talk of the frequent occasions when the rain he has brought has itself been the subject of a further petition; his parishioners often return and ask to have it stopped.

The distinctive feature of the ritual of Shinsenen's remote parishioners is the method by which the smouldering rope is carried back to the village. This they do by a relay system; the village headman runs and jogs for the first leg—as far as the north-eastern suburbs of Kyōto city—then his second in command takes over for another two-mile stretch up the hills and so on, until the least important member of the community carries the rope for the final leg within the confines of the village territory up to the spot where a further vigil is to be kept. Again, each household provides one member for the duty of running with the rope, and again, the rope must never become stationary or be put down on the ground during its journey: where it stops, there the rain will fall.

Soon after Saint Kōbō had been appointed by the Emperor to a Kyōto temple early in the ninth century, the capital and the area surrounding were hit by a drought. The priest of a sister foundation to that of Saint Kōbō received the Imperial mandate to perform rain-prayer rituals. However, his services produced no results and the command was transferred to Saint Kōbō. Now, out of professional rivalry the first priest had spirited away the dragons of the 'three thousand worlds' so that Kōbō was unable to find a single beast to appear at his calling and be instrumental in summoning up rain clouds to the sky above the spot where the prayer was being offered. However, after a two-day invocatory service, Saint Kōbō at last succeeded in finding one remaining dragon in a lake in northern India which had escaped his rival's curse; this dragon sent a serpent as its messenger to appear from the lake of the Garden of the Spirit Stream. Saint Kōbō prayed for all his might, suddenly 'sweet rain' fell, the drought was broken and the severe hardship of the farmers of the area was relieved.

One of the Shinsenen treasures still in its possession is a scroll painting just over three hundred years old. In one of a series of pictures, Saint Kōbō sits to the right in the centre of a platform surrounded by a circle of Buddhist priests, to the left is a contingent of Shintō officials, while in the centre is a pine tree at the edge of the lake. Above the pine there is a billowing black cloud and, sinewing through it, a dotted black serpent with a red-tinged underbelly and crimson red fangs. Now, in Chinese as well as Japanese belief, the dragon and the serpent are credited with the ability to summon up clouds and so to bring rain. If the dragon is black, then the clouds which it brings will be black and rain-laden. Ritual bronze vessels of the eighth century BC in China already evidence this link between the dragon and rain, for a common motif is the 'cloud and dragon' pattern.

It was to enlist the powerful support of the dragon that the villagers of Iwashimizu had gone both beyond their own boundaries and to the Zen sect priest (where one of the Shingon branch would have been less unconventional) for the reading of the sutra in front of their sacred flame. For the name of his temple was *Shinryūzan*—'Mountain of the Spirit Dragon'. They had weighed the disadvantages of the priest's not being a member of their community against the very clearly favourable circumstances of the magical potency in the very name of his temple and had decided in favour of the latter—as they had done before, for he had acted for them on the previous occasions since the war when the village had been concerned with rainmaking.

At Nachi, in the south-east tip of Wakayama Prefecture, there is still practised the relic of a fire festival which seems in origin to have been, if not a prayer for rain, at least a ritual to ensure an adequate supply of water throughout the dry summer months. Just over five miles inland, with the hills rising sharply all the way from the coast, there is an ancient shrine built into the summit of the range and shaded by sacred and venerable cedars. The shrine's fire festival—on

July 14th, at the end of the rice-planting season—takes the form of a service first at the upper shrine building; then, in the broad compound in front of the main building a procession of the shrine virgin dancers, priests and young men carrying heavy and as yet unlit pine torches forms up and winds its way down the steep and stony path through the cedars to a single *torii* gateway placed just before the base of Nachi's waterfall and always kept damp by the spray blowing from the cascade. With an unbroken drop of four hundred and thirty feet, Nachi is Japan's highest waterfall; its stream never fails, even in the driest of dry summers. The young men, dressed in loose white gowns draped up over their knees so that their legs are free to move, shoulder their heavy pine torches down to the base of the fall and, after the head priest has made his invocations and his offerings to the spirit of the water, the pine torches are lit one by one by the application of sacred fire. Then the torch-bearers clamber up and down the steep stone steps which lead to the sacred gateway at the foot of the fall: their hundred-pound weight rests over their shoulders and sparks and crackles as it flares up and sends off a thick pall of light grey smoke—which seems not unlike a summer rain-cloud—billowing up through the shade-giving cedars. Their faces soon stream with perspiration and their movements become ever more desperate as they dash their torches against the steps so that as much smoke as is possible is given off. Then, as the torches begin to splutter, they are snuffed out in water from the fall; the final overcoming of fire by water.

The Nachi festival is not a rainmaking ceremony as such, but in that it is a ritual performed to ensure that the Nachi fall, whose waters serve the farmers in the foothills and the plains below, should not fail in the parching weeks to come, this ceremony does in fact contain a number of elements familiar from rainmaking practices. One such reminiscence concerns the white robes and the conical black cap of the young stalwart who carries the pine torch, for his term for donning this costume is '*Ja wo kiru*'—'I'm putting on my serpent'—my costume designed to recall the shape and colour of the serpent, and intended to perform the serpent's function. Again, the pine torch appears constantly as a part of rainmaking, for the older a pine grows, the more do the scales on its trunk resemble those on the dragon's back.

Pine torches appear in one form of the rainmaking procedure at a village called Hirano, south of Nara. Carried round the boundaries of the community by one or two members from each household, their embers are dashed into the community pond. The name given to this procession is *kumo-yaburi*—'cloud-tearing'. If this remedy has no effect, the final resort is a huge bonfire built in the most conspicuous place in the territory farmed by Hirano, the open ground formed by the irrigation dyke system almost in the centre of the village. Again this is a community affair for each household sends straw and bamboo and, in some instances, the old wooden shelves on which the family altar rests. This is a piece of deliberate hubris: such extraordinary excess of ostentation is certain to receive its due rebuke and to provoke a reaction in the form of rain to extinguish the flames licking round these sacred objects and put an end to such sacrilege.

Such ostentation and such open attempts to draw down not only the attention but even the anger of the spirits are completely the opposite of Japanese habit. The Japanese is normally very concerned to act unobtrusively so that he may evade the calamities sent by a malignant spirit: this is one of the purposes of the battery of words in his language which tone down the baldness and increase the vague and unpointed nature of a statement; words for 'perhaps', 'probably', 'maybe' and the like are allied to a tense and conjugational system the prime purpose of which is to make more distinct not so much the time at which an action takes place as the degree of doubt or probability inherent in the action of the verb to be conjugated. The general reluctance to use a baldly pinpointing pronoun with its direct 'you' or 'I' is a further example of this normal tendency: the vague and round-about 'person in front of me' which takes the pronoun's place gives the malevolent spirit far less indication of the location of interest and so reduces the chance of spiritual retaliation in the face of undue forthrightness.

Rainmaking techniques often call for the angering of the spirits—especially those whose domain is water. A river will be dammed so that it runs dry at a spot where a dragon is thought to have his lair: mud, or the severed head of a dappled horse will be cast into a pool or put in the water at the source of a stream; such objects of particular distaste to water spirits will arouse their anger, as will the stirring up of placid pools or the floating of sacred objects such as the

A straw serpent being carried to a pool for immersion

gohei—the holy staff of Shintō—along stretches believed to be the haunts of dragons or water spirits. A huge serpent (which used to be as much as twenty, but is now usually four or five feet long) will be constructed of straw and placed in a pool. Its presence should induce that of a real serpent; its wet state should induce rain.

Not only water deities and spirits are immune from this baiting. Women climb mountains the slopes of which are open only to men and even wrestle—the height of insolence and impropriety—on the summit: burial services are held and bodies interred on holy mountains where the impure must never pollute. (These attempts to catch out a spirit are common to China, Korea and much of South-East Asia. Siamese rainmakers would expose sacred images to the sun so that they seemed almost in danger of bursting into flames: when fine weather was desired after a long spell of rain, temple roofs were torn off.) The deity believed to reside in a rock or whose image is usually represented by a stone is particularly prone to the prankish attention of the rainmaker. One village in southern Kyūshū submerged a stone deity in a pool for five days; eight men were needed to carry the rock to the pool but two could lift it after its submersion. In Wakayama, a stone Jizō (the guardian deity of children and childbirth) is sunk as far as the head in water: elsewhere it is bound tightly with ropes and submerged entirely. But one village in the northern part of the mainland, although securing the sunken stone image with ropes, is always careful to give it an occasional lift to the surface for air; too long a submersion may result in a downpour too torrential. The Jizō image may be spared the discomforts of immersion only to suffer the indignities of an overall daubing with manure—a pollution which should be effaced by an immediate fall of cleansing rain.

Two of the earliest Japanese texts extant, which were written in the first years of the eighth century, mention stones as the objects of prayers for rain. For this reason, the shrine of Isonokami, 'The Shrine Above the Stone', a very old foundation about seven miles to the south of Nara which shrine tradition claims was founded as early as the first century BC, has been intimately connected from the very first with the rain-prayers of the surrounding Yamato farmers. An alternative name often used to describe this 'Shrine Above the Stone' is Furu Shrine which derives from the River Furu flowing parallel with the shrine enclosure. Although the characters with which this *Furu* is written are different from both that for 'to shake' and the 'fall' of rain, the sound of the three words is identical.

As the shrine's chief priest blesses sacred fire in front of the spirit of the shrine's tutelary deity and it is marched round the confines and off to the particular community (the shrine serves almost fifty villages) desiring rain, the children of that community who have made a special visit to the shrine sing this song:

> *Toyoi no Tenjin,*
> *Toyoda no tabira,*
> *Ame wo furasu wa*
> *Furu no miya.*

> The Tenjin of Toyoi,
> The fish of Toyoda River,
> For making rain to fall,
> The sacred Shrine of Furu.

Toyoi, a nearby village, is famed for its shrine dedicated to Tenjin; the River Toyoda is known for its *tabira*, a rare trout-like fish, quite a delicacy, which seems to be found only in these waters; and Furu Shrine is famous for its power to create rain. Shrine records of the late sixteenth and early seventeenth centuries still preserved in its treasury show that the neighbouring farmers used to have an even better method of cashing in on the magic power of the name, for they would stand knee-deep in the waters of the Furu, cup its stream in their hands and pour it over their bodies. Thus, as well as making themselves thoroughly wet—putting themselves, that is, in just the state in which they wished their deities to put them, in the same way as many communities wear straw rain clothing for the observance of rainmaking ceremonies—these farmers were receiving their soaking from the waters of the Furu, the river with the name which sounds exactly like the word for the fall of rain which they so desired.

If rain does fall during the stipulated period for which a community has contracted to perform rainmaking ceremonies, the community proceeds immediately to fulfil all offerings vowed to its parish deity. The local gazetteer of the sub-district where Furu Shrine is situated, which records in detail both the vagaries of the weather and building developments at the shrine, indicates that there is and has for long been a close connection between the existence of drought conditions in the area and improvements on the site of the shrine. The fencing was renewed after a month's drought in 1685: early in 1796, after a long drought which began in the fifth month of the previous year and lasted through to the end of the eighth with only a slight fall of drizzle on the twenty-sixth of the seventh month, lanterns were built at the shrine. The vows of Furu Shrine's parishioners have often been fulfilled; it is not without proof of its efficacy that the shrine has held its reputation through the ages as a reliable site for rainmaking.

The gift of gratitude, often far in excess of the value of the initial benefaction and a fondness for thanksgiving and celebration are met every day in Japan. It is no good thinking that you have discharged a long overdue obligation to a Japanese friend by making him a presentation of something that you know he badly needs; he will be on your doorstep the very next morning with a return present very much more magnificent than the one you have given him. So the villagers of Iwashimizu responded in full measure to the bounty of their deity: they had vowed offerings to him and these vows they fulfilled the moment they found themselves in the position of being obliged. Then, not satisfied with this—but quite typically—they proceeded to drink their *sake* and to revel far into the night and to succeed, no doubt, in mortgaging very nearly the whole of the proceeds of the crops which their deity had just saved.

> Where are we here? Here we are before
> The gate of Yamato Shrine.
> If you look far to the east,
> Rain falls on the mountain there,
> The mountain famed for rain.
>> (Festival song of the village of Sammaiden
>> after rainfall)

The name of the mountain is 'Dragon Lord'. The village drum beats time for the lyrics—the drum once used to announce *Ban Yabure* ('Numbering is ended') as it proclaimed the finish of the emergency procedure by which such water as was available was rationed equally to each household by number. The lilt of these words, the bold voice of the singer and the joy in the chorus responses soon catch; the gay rhythm of the dance, the impelling beat of the drum and the sweep of the feet, almost cheeky and cocky, as the dancers move, are not long resistible. In these surroundings, it is hard to be a wallflower and remember the bank balance.

Seven

TENRI AND YAMATO

Sweep away the dust,
Deign to save us,
O Lord Tenri.

A huge drum, six feet tall, beats time, now missing a
syllable, now beating with the measure of the lines. As they
repeat this chant twenty-one times, familiarity distorting the
true pronunciation of the words, the four hundred Tenri
faithful move their hands in supple wristy circles. Shoeless,
they kneel and rest back on their heels on the vast floor of
bamboo matting, its odour of musty hay hanging pleasantly
on the air even though the wide shutters that line the walls
of the shrine have all been drawn back. Only one in ten does
not wear the distinctive *happi* coat of the Tenri faith; the
happi reaches to the waist and is made of a coarse cotton
material, as black as an academic gown; like the gown, the
older it gets the greener and soupier it becomes. On the back
are three characters in bold white—*Ten-ri-kyō*—'Religion
of Divine Wisdom', and characters on the lapel indicate the
believer's branch church. The bamboo matting may well constitute the largest such floor in Yamato; if it does not, some
other floor among the vast buildings of Tenri's headquarters
no doubt does, for the Japanese gape gullibly at anything
described as 'the oldest wooden gateway' or the 'tallest
concrete *torii* in the world', and Tenri's authorities are not
unaware of the pull of such rarities and lavishness. Over the
floor rises a broad tiled roof, the sweep of its slope matching
that of the thatch of the villages farther up in the hills at the

base of which Tenri nestles. The style of Japan's roofs varies considerably by locality and those of Yamato are known for the steepness of their slope which may sometimes be as acute as seventy-five degrees.

'Sweep away the dust'—the morning and evening service which these words constitute is short; after it is over the worshippers line up behind the officiating priests dressed in their ankle-length black robes and pointed and tailed, rather mysterious, black hats and hurry along polished and spotless wooden-floored corridors which twist and turn on the way to the Sanctuary of the Foundress. Then, at the end of the short prayer in honour of Miki Nakayama, the woman who founded the Tenri Sect in the 1830s, the faithful disperse and saunter back along the corridors to the main hall of worship. Some of them go on their knees again and, muttering the words 'Sweep away the dust' under their breath, repeat the pliant hand sweeps—'the dance of the hands'—that accompany them. Others, not stopping for private worship, walk straight down the steps beyond the shuttered walls of the hall to the ground-level planking that runs round the main building; they search among the neat rows for their shoes or *geta*, given a dust or polish by the *happi*-coated girls who guard them during the service, and set off, jabbering away animatedly, across the broad shingle compound to the main street of Tenri City. As they reach the steps leading down to street level, they pass the little cluster gathered round the ardent-voiced young preacher just launching himself into his five-minute talk; they turn, bow deeply in the direction of the main hall, ignore the collecting boxes of the white-robed limbless ex-servicemen and set off on the ten-minute walk down to the station.

The main street is lined with shops, five or six of which deal primarily in the literature of Tenri. There you can buy any book which the Tenri Press has published since the war— and the list is a long one—as well as the weekly newspaper devoted to the affairs of the church, the Tenri woman's magazine or one of the many children's books written and published in Tenri. A band of workers, shouldering pick or broom, swings past singing the song of 'Holy Labour' and turns into one of the hostels that each district church has built for those of its members who must stay at Tenri's headquarters; for though it began in the heart of Yamato, the centre of the world according to Miki Nakayama's teachings, the faith has spread to every corner of Japan and even to Japanese communities overseas in America, Hawaii or Brazil. The labourers have returned to the 'centre of the world' for a course of instruction in every aspect of the Tenri faith; they hear lectures on the sacred canon, they take lessons on one of the instruments that make up the orchestral accompaniment for the great festival day services on the twenty-sixth of each month, and they form a willing labour corps for the many routine cleaning chores—for dust in a Tenri building is as sinful as dust on the Tenri heart— and the construction tasks in this vast and ever-growing 'city of religion'.

At the service in the main hall there were some whose 'hand dance' was halting and not as pliant as may be; they may have been candidates who, whatever the distance of their homes from the headquarters church, must return there to hear ten lectures on the Tenri faith, its sacred books and the life of its foundress before they are accepted into full membership of the church. The candidates are not all old, nor all women; at one of such classes for candidates held early in the afternoon of a working day, one-third of the ninety people attending were men, only six of them old, and only a fifth of the women looked to be over forty. The basic doctrines that these candidates hear are that God the Parent created all men and allows them their bodies on loan; the body and the whole universe were begotten for *yōki*, joyousness, but this end is unattained when man allows dust, in the form of greed, envy, lust and the like, to cloud his heart, loaned from the Parent. Once this dust is swept and the whole world of men has effected its cleansing, all men will live at one as brothers, and as a token of the attainment of the millenium, sweet dew will fall on the stand that lies waiting for it at the heart of Tenri's hall of worship, the centre of the world.

As you step into the train, there may be members of the training course returning at the end of their three-month stay at headquarters, reluctant to leave the friends they have found from all over Japan. Those who are to remain a little longer line the platform in force, holding one end of a long gay streamer, singing one of Tenri's songs and daubing away unashamedly as the tears stream down. But by the time the electric train clatters over the points into Hirahata the tears have gone and only *yōki*, Tenri's joyousness, remains, symbolized by the flapping streamers still festooned from the train's windows.

Tenri city nestles under the hills in the heart of Yamato, the cradle of Japanese culture. About six miles to the north lies Nara, Japan's first capital and the first home of Buddhism in Japan. Less than a mile away to the east stands Isonokami Shrine, the 'Shrine Above the Stone', the supposed site of court and administration during the reign of the Emperor Sūjin in the first century BC, and the possessor of a sacred sword given, according to tradition, to the Emperor Jimmu by the Sun Goddess. To the west, about six miles away, is Hōryūji, the oldest existing Buddhist temple in Japan, built by Prince Shōtoku in AD 607. At the side of the roads which link these historic sites rise numerous tumuli reputed to be the burial mounds of many of the early emperors before the time when ruler and court selected the first fixed site for the capital at Nara.

Yamato enjoys the boon of a climate that lacks the extremes of heat and cold not infrequent in other parts of Japan. Heavy snowfalls on the wide Yamato plain are extremely rare—a fall of nine inches just over a century ago is recorded in a village diary as the wonder of a lifetime; typhoons tend to veer away and follow the lines of the surrounding hills. Almost the only intemperance in the weather to which Yamato is prone is that of drought in the dry summer months. The Yoshino, in the far south of the district, is the only sizeable river; for the rest, one can usually walk at will in their dried-up beds in late July and early August. It is not without just cause and long practice that the Isonokami

Shrine and a good number of other shrines and temples in the area have long been known for the efficacy of their rainmaking rituals.

Yamato is blessed with an almost year-round harvest of grain and fruit; in spring, there are bamboo sprouts, citron, strawberries and peaches; in summer numerous varieties of melon, pears and mushrooms; in autumn, mushrooms again, persimmon, chestnut and apples in addition to the rice harvest, while the winter orange, though perhaps less famous than its southern, Wakayama counterpart, is still no less tasty. No doubt it is because Yamato is a good place to live in that it has a long history of being lived in. The favourable nature of its climate, the rarity of natural calamities, the good soil and something of an industrious spirit in the people of Yamato all combine to justify the popular saying '*Yamato hōnen, kome kuwazu*'—'When Yamato has a bumper year, elsewhere there is no rice to eat.' This almost all-round self-sufficiency in the matter of food supplies is reflected in the marked mental independence of the man of Yamato. He does not need to call in others to help out his material livelihood, nor does he rely on them mentally. He is reluctant to ask another man for advice and it goes against the grain to help the other man or to give away to him.

Yamato has long been a land of many faiths; it is one of the areas in Japan where religious susceptibility is particularly intense. Yet the people of Nara, its administrative centre, are notoriously cold to almost any form of religion, in spite of the wealth of religious treasures, both Buddhist and Shintō, that surrounds them; so well known is this disregard as to have prompted the common jingle:

> *Kami wa kamawan*
> *Hotoke wa hottoke*
>
> Deities be damned,
> Buddha be blowed!

Almost every religion practised in Japan is well represented in Yamato and facilities for would-be worshippers are more than generous. As far as concerns Buddhism, for example, the Yamato figure for the ratio of population to temple is just half of the national average. (Yamato has one temple to three hundred inhabitants.) The most popular sects are Amidist, with their doctrine of a Pure Land in the West, attainable in return for a simple faith in the power of Amida and a repetitive invocation of his name.

Mount Ōmine, towering above Yoshino in the south of the district is the spiritual centre of a sect of mountain ascetics. As such, its slopes have long been closed to women, but four or five years ago the pupils of Nara Women's College (Buddha be blowed!), chafing at such undemocratic restrictions, ringed its foothills with pickets and did their best to penetrate a countercordon mounted by rival male undergraduates. A document of the late eighteenth century summarizes in one sentence the work of the mountain ascetic sect of Mount Ōmine: 'to pray to Inari, Fudō, Jizō and so on' (a mixture of Buddhist and Shintō deities), 'to divine about good and bad fortune and to dabble in medicine'. This is borne out by the study of the relics of a mountain priest who had a good deal to do with the Nakayama house in the years just before the origin of Tenri for, still carefully preserved in the priest's old house in a hill village overlooking the plain of Yamato, they include bamboo sticks for divination, several manuals on incantation, tracts on divination which include passages dealing with portents that indicate and explain illness, and a book on diet.

As befits a land that has been lived in for so long, Yamato is rich in distinctive local traditions. There are now only a few old people, most of them living in the hills that guard the southern approaches to the province, who remember the stories current in their childhood; but those who can are conscious of their worth and their 'Once upon a time' introductory phrases are avidly hung upon by the schoolmaster-collector of traditional tales. One of these which is particularly persistent fills a gap in Japan's creation myths for it tells of primeval floods. 'Once upon a time,' it goes, 'the whole of the Yamato reed-bearing plain was a wide, deep lake. Then, at Nijō in the north and Tatsuta in the south, cuttings were made and the lake water ran off, flowing down to the sea. Thus our Yamato came to be as we know it today, a broad plain surrounded by high hills.'

There are some indications that this local tradition is not built on pure fancy. Tatsuta, the location of the southern cutting, means literally 'dragon field'; the dragon makes his home in the water. It seems, even in historical times, that there was a lake of considerable area at the foot of the northern slopes of Mount Kagu. Now only traces of it remain, but early poets and gazetteer compilers were impressed by its size.

> In the land of Yamato the mountains cluster.
> But the best of all mountains is Kagu, dropped from heaven.
> Over the broad earth smoke-mist hovers.
> Over the broad water seagulls hover.

> *(Manyōshū* i, 2)

The folk tradition gains some support from a linguistic argument. Most of the experts agree that the original form of Yamato was *yanuto*, an Ainu word meaning lake or sea, and, however authorities may argue about the affinities of the Japanese language, it is generally admitted that in the case of vocabulary at least there were copious borrowings from the stock of Ainu words. Finally, there is a piece of ancient medical lore which indicates the presence of water. The aged grandmother will still tell you that the dojō, the loach or mudfish, swallowed whole at a single gulp, cures every kind of ailment.

One aspect of Yamato folk practice is particularly relevant to Tenri's doctrine; it is the timetable of events and ceremonies after the birth of a child. According to Yamato custom, on the seventh day after the delivery, a dish of rice boiled with red beans is prepared, prayers are said and the child is given its name. On the eleventh day, in the arms of a female relative or of the midwife who delivered it, the child pays its first visit to the parish shrine at which its parents are registered, dressed in a long quilt-like garment which is fastened at the back of the *obi*—the sash—of the woman in whose arms it is carried. Thirty days after the birth of her child, the Yamato mother purifies herself after the pollution of the delivery by taking her first bath and sits down to take her first meal at the family table. Secular purity thus attained, she must still wait another forty-five days before she is permitted to take part in any activity which brings her into contact with the *kami*, for it is not until the seventy-fifth day after the delivery of her child that the Yamato mother is regarded as sufficiently clear of contamination to visit the parish shrine. There are still not a few houses where these strict precepts are observed to the letter.

In spite of its rapid spread in the century or more since its inception, Tenri still retains almost all the characteristics that give it an unmistakable flavour of Yamato. Miki Naka-yama, Tenri's foundress, was born of and married into families with a long tradition of either service to Shintō or Buddhist devotion: in the doctrine and ritual of the sect that she created there appears much that is similar to both Shintō and Buddhism in their national and local aspects and much that might well owe its origin to local folk tradition and practice.

The most interesting of the incorporations from the latter source is the addition to the standard Japanese creation myth of a diluvial prologue based on the local stories which told of the origin of the land of Yamato. The former, as befits a people with little or no metaphysical interest or talent, is in every statement vague on the question of the shape or substance of things before creation; there was a 'chaotic mass, like an egg with no sharply defined limits', or 'a thing in the midst of the void whose shape may not be described'; or again, 'of old, when the land was young and the earth was young, it floated about as if it were floating oil'. Or, most typical, 'Before heaven and earth were produced there was something which might be compared to a cloud floating over the sea. It had no place of attachment for its root. In the midst of this a thing was generated which resembled a reed shoot when it is first produced in the mud. This became straightaway transformed into the deity Kunitoko-tachi no Mikoto.' But the Tenri creation story has none of this vagueness—though its additions and variations make for lack of clarity elsewhere: in the beginning, before the creation of man and the crystallization of earth, sea, sky and the rest, this whole world was a vast muddy lake; in it the only living creatures were primitive, undeveloped fish, the most common type of which was the *dojō*, the loach or mudfish, from which were created both the first deity and the whole of mankind. It is not very far from the loach of Yamato medical lore, the source of all healing if swallowed whole at a single gulp, to the loach of Tenri's cosmology, the seed both of *kami* and of man.

The use to which Tenri's creation story puts the Yamato observances connected with a new mother is just as interesting. Standard Japanese tradition is followed in attributing the whole of creation to the divine creator couple, Izanagi and Izanami, but details of primacy and dating are entirely peculiar to Tenri. After several deliveries that failed to survive, the female of the couple, Izanami, peopled the world in four different stages of multiple births after a pregnancy that lasted three years and three months. In the first stage, which was of seven days' duration, the land that lies between Nara and Hase (central Yamato, that is, with Tenri almost equidistant between the two termini) was populated; at the end of the next four days the rest of Yamato had received its people; during the following nineteen days Izanami gave birth to the men of Yamashiro, Kawachi and Iga, all districts which bordered on Yamato, and in the course of the final forty-five days, first the rest of Japan and then 'China and India'—the world as Miki knew it—was peopled. Now, Yamato custom in relation to the new mother calls for important ceremonies on the seventh day of the child's life (the naming ceremony), and on the eleventh day (the seven plus four, the second stage of the creation story) when it makes its first shrine visit; on the thirtieth day after her delivery (the equivalent of the third stage in the creation story) the mother becomes secularly touchable and on the seventy-fifth day (seven, four, nineteen and forty-five in the myth) she is pure for religious purposes and restrictions upon her participation in the community ritual are removed.

Tenri's debt to the mountain ascetics of Ōmine is also very plainly marked. Two of the three parts of the eighteenth century definition of the latters' work—'to divine about good and bad fortune and to dabble in medicine'—could well be used to give a fairly accurate and adequate summary of the purpose of Tenri's rituals of 'deliverance'. From the very first, Tenri used divination based on the movements of a fan, and had its 'deliverance rituals' for the treatment of illness, more especially the grant of a safe and painless childbirth and charms against smallpox. A cursory glance at the lists of early believers shows that nearly all of them first went to Tenri for the cure of some ailment and the list of authenticated cures is impressive—it ranges from mental derangement through leprosy to eye diseases and little-finger aches. And still today the most frequent purpose of enrolment for the candidates' course is in some way or other connected with illness; many high school and university converts, for example, claim that nerve or mental disorders were the impulse for their approach to the Tenri faith.

Miki Nakayama's system seems to have adopted much in the matter of detail from Shintō, such as the framework of the creation myth; a hierarchy of *kami* nearly all of them identical with those of standard belief; the pilgrimage to the 'centre of the world' as to the Shrine of the Sun Goddess at Ise, and the musical accompaniment of the service. From Buddhism came church organization; the initiation ceremony at the conclusion of the candidates' course; forms of worship and ideas about the goal of worshipful life, both of which are closely akin to those of the Pure Land sect of which Miki was at first a devout and knowledgeable member. And, at root, in its aversion from the unclean and in its definition of lapses from the proper and from the original as dust, Tenri's character is perfectly Japanese.

Sweep away the dust,
O Lord Tenri.

Eight

TABOO

The *kami* is awesome and out of the ordinary, so it is best to meet him on your own terms, with all practicable precaution taken against unplanned or unprepared encounter. Efforts to minimize the possibility of chance confrontation by the *kami* have taken a variety of forms. Conformity with the herd, the suppression of originality, is a safe negative method of avoiding the kind of notoriety that attracts the attention of the *kami* and invites them to deal suitably with what they regard as an insolent flaunting of hubris. Indirection and vagueness—as in linguistic usage—are also employed regularly as a means of manipulating those of the *kami*, for example, who personify the forces of nature. But the most widely used and the longest established preparation for contact with the *kami* consists in the strict enforcement of ritual purification and an elaborate code of taboo on actions and on persons likely to be viewed with distaste by them.

There is evidence for this stress on purificatory abstention from a time considerably before the early eighth century, when Japan's oral traditions reached written form. A Chinese account, *The Eastern Barbarians*, written in the latter part of the third century AD and part of the dynastic history of the Kingdom of Wei has this to say about the Japanese: 'When they cross the sea to visit China, they choose out a man who is not permitted to arrange his hair, does not rid himself of fleas, should allow his clothing to become filthy and does not eat meat nor approach women. This man behaves like a mourner and is called an 'abstainer'. When the voyage turns out fortunate, they present him with slaves and valuables. But if there is illness or disaster, they put this down to the abstainer's lack of scruple in his vows and put him to death.'

The professional or hereditary abstainer—a part of whose functions is now incorporated in the duties of the parish Shintō priest—appears regularly in historical times. One of the earliest Japanese texts, *Chronicles of Japan*, put into writing in the first years of the eighth century, projects into the remote past the existence of the *imibe* (*be*, a clan or corporation, and *imi*, a part of the verb 'to avoid' or 'to abstain') and incorporates the ancestor of the guild in its account of the world's first ritual impurity.

Susa-no-o, the storm-wind *kami* who 'makes green hills wither', committed all manner of unruly crimes against his elder sister, the Sun Goddess. He destroyed the channels in her rice fields, he flayed alive, and with a backward flaying, a piebald colt and he fouled her august throne in the New Palace as she was about to celebrate the feast of the first fruits. Angered by such insulting impurities, the Sun Goddess withdrew inside the Rock Cave of Heaven. Plunged in darkness, the eight myriads of the *kami* host took counsel on the most effective means of enticing her from her hiding place. Tasks were assigned to the ancestors of the several priestly corporations who shared the duties of the ritual in historical times: the ancestress of the virgin shrine dancers performed a mimic dance and the first abstainer, with another, dug up a 'five-hundred branched true *sakaki* tree'— the evergreen purifier—loaded its boughs with offerings and recited a hymn of praise. The beauty of the language and diction of this latter proved an irresistible enticement. The Sun Goddess emerged from her hiding place, her light was restored to fill the world and the *kami* host proceeded to determine an appropriate punishment for Susa-no-o. A fine (the words 'to pay' and 'to purify' are homonyms) of a thousand trays of purificatory offerings was imposed, his hair and nails were plucked out and he was banished 'downwards' from the land of the *kami*.

Nowadays, *imi*, abstention and taboo, is found most often in connection with the *kami*; but there are a great many

taboos concerned also with the crises of the life cycle, with
the most important of the year-round agricultural tasks such
as the rice planting, with other productive activities such as
hunting and fishing and with Japan's most general purifying
agents, salt, water and fire.

Taboo and abstention because of contact with the *kami*
may take several forms. One of the most widely observed is
that of pre-festival prohibition, for the person (or community) planning to welcome and entertain his deity must
have conducted himself differently from and more strictly
than is demanded by his everyday standards. The extreme
example of such pre-festival abstention is probably to be
found in the 'Taboo Festival' of a shrine in Shimane Prefecture, where, in fact, the preparatory and purificatory
abstention and the celebration of the festival itself have
merged and are no longer distinguished. Thus, this 'Taboo
Festival' is no more than a continuation of preliminary bans
on music, on all forms of sewing and needlework, on any
building or renovation of existing buildings, extending even
to the repasting of the opaque paper panes of the fragile
shōji sliding doors, and on the care and cutting of the hair
and nails. The festival day is thus one all-embracing abstention, with the door of every house in the local *kami*'s domain
tight closed against the intrusion of the unclean or the
dangerous, this safeguard reinforced by a burning torch
placed in front of each house.

Many of this series of taboos enjoined as purificatory
preparations for contact with the *kami* at his festival are to do
with food or with the impurities of blood-letting or death.
Food prohibitions concern primarily the flesh of animals; it is
common to abstain from animal flesh for seven days before
undertaking a pilgrimage to Mount Akiba in Shizuoka
Prefecture. But fruits and vegetables also figure in the taboo
lists; radish and turnip are prohibited for the three days
preceding some Buddhist celebrations. Parishioners of Gion
Shrines all over Japan eschew cucumber before their most
important celebration of the year; the reason is alleged to
derive from the similarity of the pattern of Gion's crest,

which appears on lanterns, *kimono* and the like, with that on a sliced cucumber section. This is perhaps a later rationalization of a primitive taboo the significance of which has become lost but which in origin might well have been phallic. Certainly the development of the taboo seems to have been from an earlier restriction on the offering of cucumber to the deity to a subsequent prohibition on its consumption by Gion parishioners, who became rapidly more numerous as their *kami*, at first a clan-deity local to Kyōto, became the object of nationwide worship and festival. The prohibition laid on fishing in seaside communities at the time of the annual festival of the local *kami* has undergone development from an original ban on the eating of fish by parishioners; fish is the main offering to the deity and as such should not be taken at the time of his festival by the ordinary man.

There are in addition a number of restrictions connected with 'red' and 'black' pollution which are scrupulously observed in the *komori* period immediately preceding a festival. Mention has already been made of the village near the shores of Lake Biwa where, in the event of a death within the local *kami*'s parish, no member of the whole community, whether connected with or accidentally contaminated by the deceased or not, will enter the confines of his shrine for a week. Other measures are less drastic and are restricted only to a short term prior to the festival. Thus, a village in the southern part of Kyūshū taboos for a week before the monthly celebration at its local shrine all cutting of plants or trees and any approach into the crop fields by any member in contact with the dangerous impurities of birth and death. And, again, we have described above the discrimination practised in one mountain village in central Japan where, for the annual celebration, a measure of rice is contributed by each household and the donations by any that have suffered a death or have seen an increase are scrupulously gathered and stored in separate containers.

Apart from such restrictions placed on the community as a whole, there are many instances of prohibitions on individuals who are given an important part in its ritual life. Limitations on individuals occur most commonly in the case of the year-long appointment as priest or guardian of the local shrine. There are instances where such office involves daily rising and purification before dawn, or a ban on the smoking of tobacco and the drinking of tea anywhere other than in the official's own house; in other cases he should not eat flesh or pepper, grapes or loquats or scallions; some communities demand that he take no part in mountain hunting or that he spend the entire period of his office living apart from his wife. Again near the shores of Lake Biwa, an area which seems to pay a very strict regard to the dictates of ritual purification, there is one instance, still in force, of the shrine's chief official being forbidden to shave his face throughout his tenure of the office—an interesting reminiscence of one of the third century limitations on the 'abstainer' for the duration of the long voyage to China. Similar restrictions, aimed either at the preservation of the awesome qualities transferred from the *kami* to his chief officiant or at the safeguarding of the latter from all ritual or physical stain, forbid him to touch any mud-stained farming tools or plants during the tasks of the year and oblige him to hand over the duties of his office to the previous year's shrine guardian should he be involved in any personal impurity; the predecessor, in some instances, takes over for a period of forty-nine days, an unexpected incursion of the Chinese and Buddhist seven into this national and Shintō ritual edifice.

In general, the greater part of the long list of taboos relating to the *kami* fall into one of five categories; there are restrictions on animals or fish regarded as the messengers or mounts of the *kami*, on plants or trees that have harmed or may harm them, on anything that is hateful to a particular *kami*, on types of wood and other materials used in the construction of his statue or image or to adorn his shrine and, finally, on foods that are a part of the offerings dedicated to him.

Thus, for example, there is a certain reluctance in some districts to eat shellfish; this is explained by the local belief that the fish acts as the *kami*'s courier. One community, to account for its restriction, still scrupulously observed, on the eating of octopus flesh, tells of the day when the people of a rival and nearby village came on a raid, stole the image of their patron deity and loaded it on to a boat to carry it to some out of the way hiding place; the boat was caught in a sudden storm and foundered, its precious cargo falling overboard. However, the image was soon discovered on the seabed by an octopus which took it firmly in its tentacles and brought it up safely on a part of the shore belonging to the community from which it had been stolen. So to this district the octopus is at least, if not a regular messenger of the *kami*, a very timely mount.

Almost every area has its plant or tree which, according to popular tradition, has at some time caused injury to the local *kami* and which, in deference to this tradition, is not grown generally. The most common form of these local traditions singles out for harm the *kami*'s eyes; so, in one area, even pines are not planted as a result of the harm a pine needle once did to the deity's eyes. In most occurrences of the tradition, which appears in many variant forms throughout the length of Japan, the *kami* loses only one eye, on either the stubbly branches of the tea plant or the burrs of a chestnut, on the sesame plant, or even on the spikes of a shoot of millet.

Such taboos and the popular traditions with which they are linked may well be connected with another series of popular stories which tell of one-eyed fish or snakes. One such tradition concerns a spring which rises in the compound of a mountain shrine, which never fails and the waters of which never become muddy even after the most violent rainstorm; it is the home water, primarily, of a shoal of one-eyed eels. After its conjunction with a river (the latter subject to all the hazards of summer drought and heavy rains) the fish are all perfectly normal. There are many variations in the reasons for the disfigurement of the fish detailed in such stories. In one instance, the dragon lord of a pond stole a child from a nearby village; the inhabitants angrily surged to the banks of the pond and began to hurl huge stones into the water. The dragon was hit and lost one of his eyes and, ever afterwards, the various types of fish in this pond have all been similarly imperfect. It is significant that the stretch of water, be it a small well-spring or a broad lake, central to these different traditions is almost invariably connected in some way with the ritual livelihood of its district. It may well be that, at an earlier stage, all animals and fish that were destined to become offertory gifts to the *kami* were caught and marked out as such by the removal of an eye; then they were allowed to go free once more but were thus readily distinguished when the time came to prepare the *kami*'s offering. Another village on the shores of Lake Biwa sends out specially chosen representatives to take a couple of silver carp on the day before the main festival at its parish shrine in the early part of April; one of the two is offered immediately at the shrine, but the other is put back in the lake after half of its scales have been removed. And the chosen representatives will tell you in all seriousness that when they go out the following year to catch the quota for the festival, one of the two carp in the net is invariably that marked out a year before by the removal of its scales. Japanese fishermen's stories are as tall as those of some of their English counterparts; but here there is something of an indication of the preservation, in this tradition-bound area, of an earlier custom of marking out the *kami*'s food in advance and simultaneously laying a taboo, as far as concerns general consumption and everyday use, on the victim so distinguished. It is further suggested that this practice may well be a later and less savage development of an original ritual by which the chief officials of a cult were similarly disfigured and distinguished from the ordinary person. The one-eyed man or a person with one member in place of two is awesome and out of the ordinary—the two main attributes of the *kami* nature; so the official, by virtue of his enforced participation in the *kami* nature, is ideally suited to service of the *kami*. In addition, the Japanese, with their customary vagueness in such contexts, have frequently confused server and *kami*; hence the regular appearance of old traditions concerning one-eyed deities.

Restrictions placed on the eating of one-eyed or otherwise deformed animals and fish may be a further example of the widespread taboo for general consumption, sometimes throughout the year and more often for specified periods immediately preceding the celebration of a festival, placed on anything living or inanimate, marked out as the special food of the *kami*.

Many restrictions observed locally in connection with the *kami* are stated in terms of his supposed dislikes. In most cases, the origin of such inferred *kami* whims is no longer known. In parts of the Tōhoku area, the *kami* of all Yasaka shrines dislikes wisteria so none is ever to be found within the compound of his shrines. The community deity of one village in central Japan is thought to dislike grasshoppers so not one is allowed to remain alive within the village boundaries. The domestic fowl, both cock and hen, seems to have incurred fairly widespread *kami* displeasure. In some villages not a single household will eat chicken flesh or eggs and the taboo becomes so ingrained that even young men who marry out of the village and leave it to find employment elsewhere still in many cases observe the old restrictions. The reason advanced for this prohibition appears fairly constant, though the personality about whom the story is told varies considerably; the local culture hero while sailing close inshore past the district heard a cock crow for the dawn; in fact the cock had sadly mistaken his time and the hero, hurrying through the darkness, had his oars swept away by a large wave and then, as he tried to paddle with his hand, was savaged by a shark.

Other taboos connected with the *kami* concern the type of wood used in the construction of his image; this should never be employed for secular purposes such as the manufacture of chopsticks, of shoes or of floorboarding. If dead wood is a matter for scruple, the living tree demands a deal more attentive caution. The white sandalwood, the 'graveyard tree', and the winter cherry, which is offered in Buddhist temples, are not planted inside the household compound. In other instances, there is no strict limitation on the act of planting a certain type of tree, but the tree becomes a matter for taboo as soon as it grows taller than the roof ridge; in Ishikawa Prefecture it is thought that a household will become impoverished should the branches of a maiden-hair tree overtop its roof. There is a similar fairly widespread reluctance to plant near the ordinary house trees such as the willow, the branches of which droop or hang lower than their point of junction with the trunk; Japan has a drooping cherry and plum which in certain areas (and particularly in Nagano Prefecture) are rarely seen outside the Buddhist temple compound. The tree has long been regarded in Japan as, if not possessed of the *kami* nature, at least the possible habitat of the *kami*. So the tree planted in the vicinity of a house exercises considerable influence over its destiny. Thus, if the tree withers, so will the house decay, while a tree which droops of its very nature is an open invitation to every kind of misfortune. On the other hand, a venerable and weather-beaten tree by the back door will protect a house through the gravest calamity; and since good fortune is said always to come from the south-east, in the northern part of Shikoku tall trees are often to be found in that part of the compound.

Taboos on the hunter or the fisherman while at work are world-wide. They have taken the form primarily of purification and of abstention from women prior to and for the duration of the work season. The Carrier Indians, for example, lived apart from their wives for a month before they set their bear traps and even drank from separate cups. The impulse to such caution is fear of the spirits that the hunter intends to destroy or has killed. In present-day Japan perhaps the most stringently retained of the various prohibitions laid on hunter and fisherman are taboo words. There is a long tradition of the use of a special term, often a euphemism, in place of an everyday word at extraordinary times or in specific circumstances. Among the earliest that we know are the taboo words used in connection with the Grand Shrine of the Sun Goddess at Ise. Most of the words prohibited within the confines of the Shrine or never to be mentioned in connection with it were Buddhist in origin or were derived from the 'red' or 'black' pollution. Euphemisms were found for Buddha, sutra and the like: 'death' became *naoru*, to recover; 'illness' became *yasumi*, rest, and 'blood' was replaced by *ase*, perspiration. Many of the hunter's taboo words (*yamakotoba*—mountain words) are still in common use, more particularly in the northern part of the main island. It is said that in the old days any man who forgot himself and used a word from everyday speech that was laid under taboo had water poured over his head and was sent back to his village drenched to the skin; the purification of this sudden ablution was perhaps ambivalent, for, as well as protecting the culprit from calamity sent by the offended animal that was the target of the hunt, it might also have served to lessen the insult to the quarry and made it more ready to allow itself to be caught.

The words substituted by huntsmen and fishermen of course vary with each locality and are naturally kept from prying outsiders, but they seem primarily to have to do with important necessities of life, with Japan's chief purifying agents and with the several aspects of pollution as well as with the numerous technical terms of the appropriate occupation. Thus rice is often altered to *kusa no mi*, the 'fruit of the grass', water, salt and blood are all substituted (the latter by the word *dari*—'the flow', perhaps) and the names of animals are all changed, snake becoming 'long insect' and monkey 'copper-face'. The fisherman (and often the sailor) has similar substitutions for prohibited words and terms, his 'offing words' being equivalent to the 'mountain words' of the hunter.

Salt and fire, Japan's universal detergents, the crises of the life cycle and the main tasks of the agricultural year are the subjects of frequent taboos or of a number of superstitious beliefs which are so often acted upon as to amount virtually to taboos. We have seen that fire is often 'changed'—allowed to die out and relit—after a household has been in contact with impurity; and that, in strict communities, the shrine official is rigidly debarred from lighting anything from or drinking a brew heated at any fire other than that of his own household. Strangely, night taboos are often laid on salt. After dark it becomes the subject of a word taboo, the paraphrase 'flower of the waves' being substituted for it. (But the Kyōto *geisha* will employ this euphemism at any time of the day; she is, perhaps, more than usually alive to the purificatory and ritual uses of salt, for she will often place it by her door to repel evil influences). Popular superstition enjoins a ban on borrowing or buying salt and taking it into your house at night; failure to observe the restriction invites fire.

Such popular superstitions are usually stated either in terms of a bald and outright prohibition or in the form 'if you do A, then B will happen'. The pregnant woman, as in most cultures, is hedged round with such taboos and dreads; if she drinks from the outlet of a bamboo water-pipe, then she will bear triplets; if a new roof coping is fitted to the house or if the existing one is renovated in the course of her pregnancy, her child will have six fingers and toes; if she drinks from a chipped cup or sits down on straw sacking, then her delivery will be difficult. Certain trees are often thought to attract calamity connected with the critical junctures of the life cycle. The yellow rose should not be planted in the compound of the ordinary house, for it brings infertility; bamboo, even, is an object of superstition in some quarters, as entailing death within three years of its planting; if a young person plants tea, he will die and the shrivelling up of a nut-bearing variety of yew is also a presage of death. The prickly ash brings all manner of distress; it is said to like the noise of groaning and so is avoided as attracting death, prolonged ill-health, disharmony and even snakes to any household in the compound of which it is planted.

Death and the practices that go with it are a frequent origin of superstitious taboo. The corpse is laid in state with its 'pillow' (i.e. the head) facing the north; as a result there is a general reluctance to lay out the clothes of the living with the upper part—the neck of a jacket or the waistband of trousers and so on—lying towards the north; and misfortune comes if you leave a kettle with its spout turned towards the north. In Iwate Prefecture contact with death through attendance at a funeral or entry into the house of the dead person should entail a strict enforcement of absence from any field where crops are growing for a week from the third day after contagion; if you are in the middle of work which cannot be allowed to lapse for a whole week, then you should have a deputy attend and suffer infection in your stead.

The evil consequences of the 'north-facing pillow' apply also to some of the major tasks of the farmer's year. If, after reaping, the stalks of corn are left to dry with the ears facing north, long and heavy rains will fall and will hinder the progress of the harvest. There are a great many prohibitions laid on the farmer where illness is threatened in the event of violation. So, for example, if you enter the paddy on the forty-ninth day after sowing or planting, you will lose your sight; entry into the rice fields on the fifth day of the fifth month incurs the threat of disease in the legs or feet and all manner of illness will ensue if, in the course of the rice transplanting, the direction of the rows is altered. Nor are the farmer's tools or household utensils immune from this type of superstition; the gift of a ladle to children as a toy renders the donor liable to epilepsy.

There is a whole battery of superstitions concerning age, for there still remain widely held and strongly persistent beliefs that certain years are calamitous. These beliefs, in the main, seem to have originated in Japan and in the Ryūkyūs. The most calamitous of the evil years according to Japanese belief are, for women, thirty-three and, for men, forty-two. These are normally explained by recourse to a theory of a play on homonyms, for '*sanzan*'—thirty-three—may also mean 'birth difficulty' and '*shi ni*'—forty-two—is identical in sound with 'to death'. This is by no means our first encounter with such magic plays on words; but in this instance this line of explanation seems not quite to clinch and to contain something of a taste of later rationalization. It might be better to give some account of the nature of these superstitions and of the measures taken to counteract the anticipated calamities before attempting an explanation.

Steps are taken to avert evil at the very start of the dangerous year, or even at the beginning of the previous year, for it is often held that the calamity may extend both to the year preceding and to that following the harmful period itself. The person entering on an evil season will go to his parish *kami*'s shrine to ask for aid and protection and on the way there will drop a personal possession such as a comb, a needle, a hair ornament, or something less closely associated with him such as a coin, at a crossroads; this practice is called 'calamity dropping'. The choice of a busy place will ensure that the potential evil is worn off or spread by the many who pass by. There is significance in the general preference for the comb as the possession best discarded in this manner. In the creation story, the first male used the teeth of his comb as torches on his visit to the Land of Darkness in search of his wife; it provided protection against the pollution of the land of the dead as well as mere light in the darkness. There are a number of popular taboos and good luck theories connected with the comb; it is a good omen if a woman unwittingly drops one at the lunar new year; there is a fairly general dislike of receiving a comb as a present or of picking one up from the ground. And, most interesting in the context of the complex of beliefs in calamitous years, the action of throwing a comb is said to sever the link between man and wife or the bonds of blood relationship. So the man who drops a comb hopes thereby to break the ties between himself and the calamities of an evil year. He may also hope to secure the assistance of a magic play on homonyms, for the hair of the head, *kami*, with which the comb is closely associated, has the same sound as the word for deity; or again, the deliberate loss of the comb may signify the loser's intention to enter a period of scrupulous purification; in some instances this entails permitting the beard to go unshaven and the hair unkempt.

Other measures adopted to ward off the calamity of a dangerous year included a pilgrimage to some mountain or shrine—very often that of the Sun Goddess at Ise—or to a Buddhist temple; sometimes these pilgrimages or a period of *komori* in a shrine were undertaken for three successive years

—those preceding and following in addition to the actual bad year. Then there were the tricks which helped, to all outward appearances, to evade or by-pass the fateful years; New Year celebrations might be observed twice, or two New Year offertory shelves might be set up in place of the usual one—in such circumstances the dual New Year system, with a secondary 'Little New Year' celebrated at the full moon of the first month, could be turned to excellent advantage. Or the assistance of red, the magic and traditionally lucky colour, might be invoked. The Japanese male, whatever his age and whatever the season, has a preference for long baggy underwear; if he is forty-two he still often changes the normal off-white to red!

The ills of the dangerous years are alarmingly contagious if not kept in check by careful purification and safeguard. We have seen already that calamity is believed to be liable to spread to the years before and after the central calamitous twelvemonth. It may also extend to children born to parents undergoing the stresses of a dangerous year; to such an offspring the name 'calamity' or 'devil child' is often given, though it is sometimes thought that the child of the opposite sex to that of the parent who is in the dangerous years, by virtue of this sex difference, will escape the curse. Like the farm animals of the man involved in 'black' uncleanliness, such children are often given over in temporary adoption— which may only last for a few moments—to a near neighbour or a handy relative. If the latter's kinship is through the mother, the child thus going to a house with a different surname, so much the better; for a further means of diverting the contagion from such an infant is to give it another surname, or a different given name, or even to pronounce the characters for the latter with a phonetic other than the usual. This last method is not so difficult to effect as may appear; most Chinese characters have in Japan at least two possible renderings, the one an approximation to the Chinese pronunciation at the time and of the locality of the loan, the other that of the indigenous word to which the character was applied. So a name compounded of two characters is usually capable of four quite distinct renderings. Nor is this the end of the matter; most old-fashioned houses have their long observed traditions which often require quite personal and eccentric phonetic equivalents for a character which must always form part of the given name of its male members. One scion of such a household, now in his middle thirties, rejoices in the personal name of 'Beautiful Capital'—he was conceived in Paris! But because of this family tradition, the characters for 'beautiful' and 'capital' are applied to a phonetic completely different from any that might reasonably be expected.

There is a clue to the derivation of these superstitions about the dangerous ages in the Japanese belief that contamination is most liable to spread to acquaintances, neighbours and relatives of the same age as the person originally polluted. So, often, on the death of a classmate at school whose age is the same as yours, especially if you happen to be in the course of a dangerous year, you make yourself scarce and stay as far away as may be from his house and the last rites in his honour. Grouping by age and the practice of allowing or withdrawing certain privileges to an entire group in accordance with age rather than after assessing the merits of the individual are both old-established features in Japan. They may well provide a satisfactory account of *Shichi-go-san*, the 'Seven-Five-Three Festival' as well as of the edifice of superstitions built round the theory of the dangerous years. The former, the 'Seven-Five-Three Festival', is now observed most generally on the fifteenth of the eleventh month when children of seven, five and three years go along dressed in their best festival clothes to the parish shrine, to express their and their parents' gratitude to the *kami* that the appropriate age has been reached in safety. But November 15th is not the sole day for the observance of this celebration; certain communities include it as a part of the annual festival of their parish deity and others make it one of the long list of New Year rites. The latter practice is instructive, for the ritual then becomes an act of gratitude for the safe attainment of the objective and an invocation of future protection at the very time when the goal is obtained.

Now it is suggested that the word 'dangerous'—*yaku*—in 'dangerous years', homonymous with a word meaning 'duty' or 'service', is yet another example of the magic play on identically sounding words. The type of 'service' intended by the term is that of the *kami*, contact with whom, in spite of a scrupulous attention to all the details of the rules for purification, is liable to be dangerous not only to the individual in question but to all within his circle or connected with him in any way, as by an identity of age. By this explanation a reasonable account can be given of the 'Seven-Five-Three' ceremonies, for there are still examples where the attainment of these ages brings eligibility to hold office or to perform duties connected with the service of the *kami*. At a shrine on the island of Awaji, which sprawls across the Inland Sea south-west from Kōbe almost to Naruto on the north-east tip of Shikoku, children who have attained the age of three have prominence in one of the annual ceremonies called 'Flower Tower'. Loaded into chairs carried on the shoulders of lusty young parishioners, they precede the *mikoshi* and, as the official pages of the festival, on whom rigid purificatory rites are enjoined, they head a long procession of worshippers making for the shrine.

The age of five is also significant, though not so frequently as three or seven, in some ritual observances. At Matsuno-o Shrine, a few miles west of Kōyto, children of five and seven are the central figures of a ceremony performed in late July to mark the end of and to bless the rice-planting. Girls dressed in green and boys in a dark purple, the children congregate in the parish shrine ready for a beauty contest judged by the chief priest; the one elected as the bonniest baby is hoisted on the shoulders of the village headman and leads a procession of the rest, similarly carried, round every paddy field in the community's territory. The chosen child casts a rice shoot into each field, this shoot ensuring the beauty and richness of the crop that will grow there.

Seven, for both boys and girls, marks the end of infancy. Until that age they are regarded as the '*kami*'s children' and any child who dies before attaining it is not buried in a proper tomb in the appropriate graveyard but in a grave dug within the household compound. But at seven years of age the child gains its first privileges (and thereby incurs duties and obligations) on the way to full membership of the community; it becomes one of the parishioners of the community *kami* and its name is recorded in the roll of inhabitants. Formerly, at the age of seven, the child's topknot was cut; perhaps this was a measure to ensure the ritual cleansing of all the pollution that had accumulated in the years previous.

Thus the ages of three, five and seven all indicate a step on the way to full citizenship of the community and full responsibility for service of the parish *kami*. Most of the calamitous years also coincide with the year of assumption of new and greater duties in the service of the community and its *kami*. At the age of forty-two, at an earlier stage of Japan's development, a man was deemed to have left the young men's group and was regarded as worthy of joining the association of the 'middle-old' or even the elders. As such, he would become eligible for much more weighty tasks at the parish shrine. At a shrine in Toyama Prefecture it used to be the practice for men who had just attained the age of forty-two to carry the *mikoshi* at the shrine's main annual festival, and all males aged forty-two on the island of Okinoshima act as servers at the island shrine. Sixty-one, another of the widely dreaded dangerous years in the case of the male, is traditionally the age when a man ceases to be liable for public duties in the village and becomes free to devote his time and energy to the more weighty tasks in the matter of community rites and parish festivals for which he is now eligible.

So, for the male, most of the dangerous years coincide with the commencement of new liabilities and responsibilities in the service of the *kami*. This may have been the case formerly with the dangerous years of the female—commonly held to be nineteen and, though less often, thirty-seven as well as the thirty-three noted above; but there is now no trace of what such new eligibility might have been. The only suggestion that the Japanese can offer is that the woman, in their eyes, reaches her full bloom at the age of thirty-three (the most dreaded of the three dangerous years for the woman); she would be also, in that case, most open to the contamination of the 'red' pollution at that age. If the dangerous years coincide in fact with the assumption of new religious functions, then closer contact with the *kami* results in a transfer of a greater degree of *kami* potentiality and nature to the officiant; he thus becomes a source of danger not only to others but even to himself.

The Japanese word used most generally for purification is Buddhist in origin and signified the single-minded pursuit of the faith until it was twisted to apply to this pre-eminently Shintō passion for purity. None the less, the Japanese pursuit of purification has been and remains eminently single-minded. The type of ceremony which this urge to ritual cleanliness might be expected to produce does in fact still exist—the festival in which, for fear of contamination, no one dares do anything. On the twenty-fourth and twenty-fifth of the first month, the people of the Isles of Izu celebrate their 'taboo day' and for the entire twenty-four hour period stay inactive, and so uncontaminated, behind firmly bolted doors.

Nine

THE VILLAGE YEAR

We have ranged over Japan in search of some of the highlights among her customs, both individual and group. Now, it would be well to narrow the sights to a single community in order to fashion the links and to fill the gaps between these highlights and to give a general picture of its year-round activities and ceremonies.

Okinoshima—the Island in the Offing—lies just over a mile from the east shore and roughly midway between the north and south limits of Lake Biwa. Slightly more than seven miles in circumference, it is a rare example of an inhabited lake island. The harbour nestles at the south-east shore between the two abruptly rising hills which constitute the island and offer shelter from the winds which in winter and late into the spring blow cold and strong from the mountains to the north. Almost all the hundred and fifty houses which constitute the Okinoshima community snuggle close to the lake and the harbour, partly for protection from the weather and partly for convenience, for the island has no wells and all water, whether for drinking or for washing, comes from the lake. This, with the infrequency with which the fisherman takes his meals, may well be one of the causes of the prevalence of liver ailments on the island.

The concreted paths that run among these houses are dark and narrow and there is scarcely room for three to walk abreast even on the main pathway that crosses the community from the foot of the steps below the shrine building to those leading up to the school, via post office and headquarters of the fishermen's co-operative. Naturally, these paths are too narrow to take a motor car or even a three-wheeled truck; there are no motor bikes, the latest teenage craze, on the island and in fact the only wheeled vehicles that it boasts, two bicycles, never leave the school playground where they serve to train pupils in the ways of the mainland should they ever decide to leave the island. Bereft of his cycle, and even his trolley, the bean-curd man peddles his wares in a box carried on his head. The island musters six shops, two tobacconists (little more than a glass display case and a cash drawer in the front room, open only when grandma feels like it), two general stores, open from 6 a.m. to 10.30 p.m. and dealing in everything from medicines to frying pans and whisky, a barber's shop and a *sake* store. It is significant that of these only the owner of the last makes a living without combining farming or fishing with his labours as a trader. These fishermen drink as hard as any, according to those who transport the *sake* from the mainland; a good catch is almost always the signal for a long night out.

One of the most striking and endearing aspects of Okinoshima is the calm and the gentle tempo of life as these islanders live it. There is an almost complete absence of the clangour that comes from the abuse of the modern or the western; even the radio sets, though, like others in Japan, left on all through the day, are yet tuned so low as to be only rarely heard outside the open front shutters; the pop-pop-pop of the motorized boats, heard from a distance, dissolves dreamily in the slender gauze of the haze that softens the starkness of the hills beyond the water. And the island has no dog or cat—with the result that the size and the quantity of its rats have attracted many a zoologist from the remote ends of Japan.

Island tradition has it that the first settlers were defeated warriors of the Minamoto armies who sought shelter here at the end of the twelfth century; certainly the names of these warriors account for seven of the dozen or so which are shared by the eight hundred islanders. The leader of the warrior group, one Minami, gave his name to a clan which, even in the memory of a man only in his early seventies

today, was the most flourishing on the island but which has
been dogged through the last two generations by a succession
of girl births and early male deaths.

Fishing is the basis of Okinoshima's economy. Almost
every native island household owns its small fishing boat
and every native family, even one with a female head or a
branch house founded by a second or third son, has an equal
share in the island's fishing and hill forest rights. As well as
these small private boats, there are two large fishing smacks,
each manned by thirty fishermen and owned by the fishing
co-operative. These fish by dragging, usually to one of a
dozen or so points on the eastern shore of the lake opposite
the island. The choice of the dragging site is an art which
takes a long time to learn, governed by the state of the wind,
currents, the temperature of the water, the moon (the degree
of light affects fish movements) and the volume of recent
rain. There is, of course, a rich store of lore concerned with
the expertise of the fisherman; salmon-trout, for instance,
congregate near river estuaries on rainy mornings in spring
and early summer.

Today there is a broad division of labour according to sex,
the men fishing and the women working in the paddy fields
owned by the island on the mainland to the east. But this has
not always been the case; the few husband and wife teams
still fishing today are in fact far more in accord with traditional fishing methods. To understand the reason for the
change one must go back a little in island history. The fishing
waters to which Okinoshima had sole rights for almost four
hundred years were strictly defined early in the second half of
the sixteenth century and have since been jealously guarded
against all infringement. This has come, more often than not,
from Katata, the traditional rival, a fishing community over
on the western shore of Lake Biwa. This rivalry led to raids
on the other's settlement and to poaching in his waters; after
the worst clash in the early 1770s, complaints by both sides
led to litigation in the courts in Kyōto which dragged on for
eight years and completely exhausted the resources of both
parties. Now, with all such preserves and privileges abolished

by occupation democracy, there is no scope for such argument, but it still happens that few alien boats fish traditional island waters or, more particularly, drag their nets to the mainland coastal sites that were formerly reserved for the island fishermen. The feud of the past has long been patched up to the degree that Katata's boatbuilders, with the distinctive metal-patterned prow of their product, act as the island's sole manufacturers.

In the last years of the nineteenth century and until the late 1920s Katata must have counted itself fortunate in its change of role from major rival fishing community to boat supplier for in those years came a development which was to have significant influence in broadening the basis of the island's economy. Post-Restoration modernization called, above all else, for stone, for railway tracks, for water conservation and control projects, and for the western-style buildings that began to appear in the urban centres to the south-west, such as Kyōto and Ōsaka. Okinoshima was able to provide both the stone and the means of transport for these enterprises, water transport being at the time both the most economical as well as the most convenient. At one stage in the years just after the turn of the century, when the sector of the trunk railway line on the mainland opposite was being laid, there were as many as a hundred and fifty islanders (of a total population of a little over six hundred) engaged in quarrying and fashioning stone, and over forty large-type transport boats, capable of holding three to five hundred bushels, were kept busy.

This flourishing trade in stone brought with it considerable changes in the island's economy and way of life, for with the income that came from this source the islanders were able to buy paddy on the mainland to the east. Hitherto, only a mere five acres or so had been cultivated, part on the island itself and part on this eastern coastline of the lake. There being scarcely space between the tightly packed houses for even a small plot of vegetable *hatake*, a spirited fish-wives' squabble used to occur whenever, in summer, one of the transport boats brought back a load of eggplant or cucumber from the mainland. But with the acquisition of more than seventy acres of mainland paddy in the late 1880s, it came about that the islanders could produce almost all their vegetables and about four-fifths of their rice requirements. During and after the Pacific War, the stone industry declined. One of the chief factors in this decline has been the rapid development in the post-war period of the much cheaper truck transportation. Stone for the new building in Kyōto and bomb-ravaged Ōsaka and Kōbe is now quarried nearer to the building sites. Today there are only five or six Okinoshima families engaged in the stone industry, these among the poorest in the whole community—where there were thirty to forty in the years just before the war.

But the benefits brought by this short-lived stone industry have remained, with the result that agriculture has come to play an integral part in the life and economy of the island. This is evidenced by the usual provisions made for a second son when he sets up a branch household within the island, for it has become traditional to start him out with a boat, a house and one *tan* (about a quarter of an acre) of paddy, 'so that he may have rice to eat'. Yet farming is very much a secondary occupation, with yields only about a quarter of the average for the whole district. This, the men claim, is partly because farming is relegated to the women; it is partly because the long trip by boat to the fields means the loss of working time and again because the island women are not naturally or originally farmers. Every morning at about eight o'clock, once breakfast has been cleared and the house tidied, the womenfolk gather at the harbour and cross to the mainland paddies, returning in time to heat the water for the bath and prepare the evening meal. The gentle and leisurely pace of life as these islanders live it is expressed perhaps at its most distinct in their agricultural labours, for even in the midst of the busiest season in the farmer's year, in early June when the *mugi* harvest is in full swing and the rice transplanting is just beginning, the farming contingent does not leave the island until its regular eight o'clock and returns no later than usual, often leaving behind on the island not a few perfectly able-bodied grandfathers. Grandparents and babies take over the island until the fishing boats come back in the middle of the afternoon. You would have to go far to find so many grandfathers dandling grandchildren above the harbour wall and making quite a good job of being day-nurses.

The Okinoshima community is a very tightly-knit, inward-looking and closed society. As has been said, the eight hundred islanders share a mere dozen surnames; the houses are so closely clustered together as to make any geographical division of upper and lower or east and west meaningless, and there is no consciousness of social or financial division. Each household, provided it possesses the sole qualification of island birth, has identical privileges and powers in the matter of fishing, quarrying and hill forest rights. There are, per-haps, four or five individuals who stand out from the rest; the postmaster, who is justly proud of his two-volume work, written in a flowing yet firm hand, *Okinoshima Monogatari*— The Tale of Okinoshima; one of the two Buddhist priests and his schoolmaster son-in-law; and the head of the fishing co-operative, an office which rotates each year and is elective.

This equality of privilege and status within the island has no doubt assisted the development of the islanders' sense of self-sufficiency as a group. Marriage is contracted almost entirely between islanders; in the last thirty years only five men have taken wives from the mainland and these departures from standard practice are so distinctive that the merest hint of the question, 'Who has married outside?' prompts a rapid and unhesitating enumeration of these five names. The list is given in terms of personal rather than family names for it is island practice to use the former on all but the most formal occasions. Foreign, that is mainland wives, ill-trained for the specialist tasks that are required of them, are not an eco-nomical proposition. There has not been one since the end of the war.

Nor, until very recently, have the islanders looked to the mainland either for further education or for employment. Okinoshima has still to produce its first undergraduate and it is very rare to find even a boy, much less a girl, carrying on

with his schooling at a mainland high school after com-
pleting his years at the island's middle school. On the other
hand, in the last few years there has been a marked increase
in the number of school leavers who seek employment on the
mainland. Of forty-seven in the period 1950-2, only eight
left the island; but during the period 1953-5, nineteen of
forty-two went to find work on the mainland. At the end of
the school year in March 1960, the number of those who left
the island, eight, for the first time topped that of those who
stayed, seven. Such new trends are in open defiance of the
tradition that the island's female deity, Himenomikoto, is so
jealous of her charges that she ensures that, should any of them
escape from her clutches and cross to the mainland to seek a
living there, he will inevitably meet with ill-fortune. So far,
none of these adventurous young people has failed—or at
least none has openly admitted failure by returning.

Okinoshima, then, a closed society, openly distrustful of
all outsiders, with few who leave returning to spread the
sedition of mainland knowledge, and with a mere twelve
television receivers, is a folklorist's paradise, in spite of the
devoted adherence of all its hundred and fifty households to
the Shin sect of Buddhism, so often elsewhere in Japan the
effacer of custom and tradition.

Much of the lore and taboo has to do with the fishing
industry. The tides and currents of Lake Biwa are affected
most by the wind, by the state of the rivers that empty into it
and by the volume of rainfall. So it is not unnatural that much
of the weather lore concerns the wind; thus, for example, a
south-west wind in March or April ushers in a long spell of
fine weather; a north wind on a spring night again portends
good weather while rain in May—called *uojima*—is a prelude
to very full nets and on such occasions the large co-operative
boats drag their nets two and sometimes three times an
outing.

The movements of the fishermen are not restricted by as
many superstitions and taboos as one might expect in the
case of a community earning the best part of its livelihood
from the capture and killing of a living thing; perhaps the

fact of the constant proximity of water, even though it lacks salt content, is regarded as a sufficient purifier of the pollution involved in killing. Pumpkins and the whey from bean-curd are taboo for one about to go out fishing. The fisherman will only take black sheat-fish; red and yellow varieties, said to be sacred to Benzaiten, the goddess of fortune, are put back into the water and even if they are taken, the goddess is thought of as scheming for their escape. There is a small shrine sacred to Benzaiten on the island, on the edge of the bay beyond the most easterly of the houses in the village. This shrine used to be part of the processional route of the main island festival, but it is now only very rarely visited, except on its own festival day in the middle of October. It has the reputation of being a copious rain-producer, but this benefit has not been required since the end of the war.

There is now only one remaining *oki kotoba*—'offing word' —a word not to be used while at work on the lake, but even this last relic is not widely known or practised. The word is *bonsan*, a Buddhist priest. In that the majority of taboo words with a religious connection are related to Shintō, this sole remnant is another indication of the wholehearted devotion to Buddhism in the area.

On the tenth of every month the fishermen offer prayers to *Kompira San*, their guardian deity. There is more elaborate attention to his cult on New Year's Eve when a pine branch is set up in the live-well of every boat that is to engage in fishing in the coming year and sweet *sake* and *mochi* are offered to him.

But it is the Little New Year, January 15th, rather than New Year's Day that is used by Okinoshima to mark the majority of administrative or social changes. The new chief of the fishermen's co-operative, for instance, enters office on Little New Year's Day and the complements of the co-operative's two drag-fishing boats are chosen on the previous day, making their first fishing expedition together on the morning of the Little New Year. Selection is by lot, conducted every other year, one member from roughly half of the island's fishing households serving for a term of two years and then standing down for a similar period. The lot is strictly personal and is not transferable. Should any to whom it falls not wish to take advantage of his fortune, he is not permitted to transmit his share even within his immediate family, to son or brother, for example, but must make way for the next on a reserve short list. Surprisingly, there are not a few lone-wolves who do forgo this chance; individualism counts for a lot on this island and principle is strong enough to counter the hope of reward, for co-operative fishing, on the whole, brings greater returns than individual effort.

As might be expected, there are several unique and distinctive features in the marriage customs of this closed community. Selection is natural, with no enforced or conventional visiting or 'viewing' of the prospective mate. Go-betweens or investigators could perform little useful function in a group of only a hundred and fifty families where marriage is almost invariably within the island and most people, if they do not know outright, can make a shrewd guess about the affairs and fortunes of the rest. Once the couple have made their decision to marry, the arrangements are entirely in the hands of the women of the two families concerned. The men even succeed in avoiding the ceremony itself; women members of the bride's household carry her luggage to her new home where the simplest of ceremonies is conducted, this lacking even the traditional sips of *sake* by bride and bride-groom. The latter, at the time of the ceremony, joins his and his bride's immediate male relatives in some discreetly out of the way house and is the guest of honour at a wedding day stag party. The sole male intrusion on the scene used to be the throwing of mud from the harbour bottom at the bridal procession by jealous and disappointed young men unrelated to either of the bridal pair. Naturally, the bride goes without her husband—who is either out fishing or asleep after his return from a night's fishing work—when she makes the formal journey back to the home of her parents on the third day after her wedding.

Brides of first sons invariably live with their husband's parents, joining in the farming labours and often helping to man the household fishing boat. When the older couple retire—and retirement comes at a tender age, often even in the early sixties, on this island—they withdraw almost completely from their rights and privileges as household head. The household's share in fishing, timber and stone rights is made over to the eldest son who also inherits the place in the lottery which decides the complement of the co-operative fishing boats. The parents even vacate their room of honour on the ground floor of their home, the *nando*, next to the room which houses the household's Buddhist altar, and move upstairs to what has now become known as 'the retirement room', *inkyo*. A century ago, this space beneath the roof was used to store fishing tackle, nets, brushwood and kindling for the bath fire.

The 'move upstairs' in Okinoshima is, in fact, the signal for withdrawal from almost all productive activity. One 'retired' grandfather, who looked older than the sixty-three to which he admitted, summed up the gentle and leisurely pace of life on this island when, rocking and swinging his whimpering grandson on his back at every pause between phrases, he described his day. 'Oh, I have a good read through the paper once she's gone' (a reference to his daughter-in-law leaving on the boat for the paddy fields) 'and I've got the house to myself. I might take a boat out there,' pointing to the blue bay beyond the harbour, 'and fish for an hour or two for pleasure. For pleasure, mind you.' There was a heavy stress on the repeated words. 'And I take the grand-children for a stroll. But I've not set foot in our paddy for years, even at planting time or harvest. And I fish only for pleasure.'

There are few pregnancy taboos and superstitions. If an expectant mother's face is drawn and lined, she will bear a boy; if she sees an outbreak of fire during her pregnancy, her child is likely to be disfigured by birthmarks. No food taboos are observed today and none are remembered by older residents. The afterbirth, which is carefully guarded from exposure to the sun, for fear of polluting the latter, is buried in a corner within the compound in the case of a boy and in ground just beyond the shadow of the house eaves in the case of a girl; this will induce and ensure her departure from the house when she reaches marriageable age. A still birth is known by the name 'water baby'.

On the seventh day after the delivery is removed one of the layers of straw sacking on which the mother lies and which prevent the spread of the contamination of the birth beyond the confinement room. The second layer is taken up on the twentieth day, at which all taboos on the delivery room are lifted, and the sacking is then purified by the application of ash. For some time after her delivery the new mother is not allowed to eat any fish with blue backs; it is suggested that as the lake water is blue, this identity of colour might lead to her next confinement ending in the delivery of a 'water baby'. The new mother also avoids both salmon-trout and eel, the reason given being that both of these have an excess of fat tissue. A baby boy is regarded as being sufficiently clear of pollution to make his first visit to the island deity's shrine on his thirty-first day; a girl must wait for this ritual purity for a further two days.

After a death, close relatives of the dead person abstain from all form of fish until the end of the period of pollution. The last rites are followed immediately by salt purification both of all relatives and helpers who have had contact with the dead and of the place of burial or the cremation site. Cremation is by far the more common method of disposal, for the general rule on the island is that where the dead person has used his voice, he is cremated; only a child that dies at birth before its first cry is buried. Taboos on the relatives of the dead are stricter even than for those who have been in contact with the 'red' pollution; this is another instance of the hold of Shin Buddhism on the island people. Men are prohibited for forty-nine days and women for thirty-five days from visiting the island shrine or from taking fish from the lake. The fact that similar restrictions do not extend to the other two island occupations, farming and stone hewing or transportation, indicates the relative respect in which the islanders hold their most traditional and most profitable occupation.

Its sacred buildings, together with the headquarters of the fisherman's co-operative and the newly-rebuilt school, are the island's most conspicuous. Among the sacred buildings, there are, first, two Shin sect temples, one of which was at first a Tendai foundation; the island thus, at one time, typified the two main Buddhist influences in the area for while the Tendai sect is the strongest in the mountain valleys west of Lake Biwa, the rich plainland to the east of the lake is dominated by the Shin sect. The roofs of these two temples soar high above the *inkyo* of the houses clustered underneath them; as the tiny ferry boat bobbles and sputters into the choppy water beyond the lee of the headland sheltering Chōmeiji, the mainland harbour from which Okinoshima is reached, these temple roofs are easily the most outstanding landmarks and give a reminder of the aptness of the phrase of the priest of a village not far away to the east—'Seek out the highest roof in the village, and you can be sure that it covers the worship of Shinran.' There used to be six days in the year when the faithful made pilgrimages to their temple and, as a congregation, took part in a service. These holy days, however, are now ignored by the young people on the island and the temple is attended at such times by only a few of the oldest inhabitants. The same fate has befallen an old religious holiday, celebrated for four days at the end of January; very few fishermen now take time off from their work to observe this ritual. With the construction of new administrative buildings, such as the co-operative centre, certain activities that once had religious overtones have now become secularized. The fishing co-operative lottery, now conducted in the administrative building, used to be held alternately in the main hall of the two temples. In much the same way, it will be remembered, the vigil in Iwashimizu's rainmaking ceremonies, once conducted in the village shrine, has been transferred to the main room of the Agricultural Advisory Hall.

The island has three Shintō shrines. That sacred to Benzaiten, with its conspicuous vermilion *torii*, stands at the foot of the eastern slopes of the more northerly hill. The other two both look down across the harbour and the settlement round it from a grove of cherry trees midway up the eastern slope of the southern hill. The higher of the two is a sanctuary of the *yama no kami*, the mountain spirit, and the fluctuations in the fate of this deity, worshipped by the island's stone labourers and transporters, are a very accurate index to the history of the stone industry itself. Built in the first years of this century, when the demand for Okinoshima stone was nearing its peak, the sumptuous and lavish construction is quite out of keeping with the natural simplicity of other such sanctuaries sacred to this *kami*. At first this shrine had its separate parishioners who celebrated the festivals of their deity independently, one of them, the spring festival on May 9th, even being accorded the rare honour of an island holiday when even fishermen rested for the whole day. Now, after the decline of the stone trade, the sanctuary, kept in order by the officiants of the island shrine just below, is not the scene of any of the community's year-round ceremonies and is never the goal of a special visit by any of the few remaining households that engage in stone work. Its festivals, once important events in the ceremonial calendar, have now become mere appendages to those of the island's patron deity, their entire significance lost. As has been explained above, the mountain spirit fulfils a dual role, becoming the *ta no kami*, the paddy spirit, for the rice growing season. At times of transformation he is escorted from the one domain to the other. It seems that a relic of a ceremony of this nature is still observed in Okinoshima. The rare holiday on May 9th takes the form of a leisurely day-long picnic on the upper slopes of the higher of the two hills. The name given to this outing is *Go-en*, a bond, a tie, presumably with the stone hewers' mountain spirit. It may well be that at this time of the year the Okinoshima mountain spirit was about to assume his other manifestation, and that this climb to the hills was originally for the purpose of escorting him down to the plains to supervise the rice crop. But none of the islanders has attempted to explain this excursion in terms of a ritual connected with the worship of the mountain spirit and all

view their outing purely as a pleasure trip, even postmaster
Nishii interpreting it in terms of the beauty of the azaleas
which are just then in full bloom at the summit of the hill.

Just below this sanctuary of the mountain spirit is the
shrine of Himenomikoto, the island's patron deity and a very
rare example of a female parish *kami*. The shrine sponsors the
island's spring and autumn festivals, two of the main celebrations in the year-round ceremonial. The spring festival,
celebrated on May 8th, takes on almost the aspect of an
'island day', the day on which new buildings are officially
opened, new projects inaugurated. So, in 1928, when elec-
tricity was brought to the island, it was on May 8th that the
current was first switched on.

Until the spring of 1944 the island deity's *mikoshi*, portable
ark, used to be taken on a real *watari* (literally, a crossing), a
journey from home shrine to small outlying sanctuary. But in
that year there occurred some accident, which no one on the
island cares to go into in detail (after viewing even the considerably sobered recent ceremonial, one suspects a certain
degree of overpatronization of the *sake* shop). Whatever the
nature or the explanation of the mishap, both boat and
mikoshi sank and the spring festival was celebrated in a much
abridged fashion for more than ten years until a new *mikoshi*
was completed in 1956. Far greater care is taken of this
larger and more magnificent ark and it is not entrusted even
to the newest and most lake-worthy boat. The trip over the
water has been replaced by an overland journey; the ark is
borne on the shoulders of young male parishioners the length
of the island's main pathway. Even so, the journey involves
not inconsiderable risks, for these young men have already
drunk well and appear to be no exception to the spirit of
lustiness and rough vigour which characterizes all festivals in
the area in general; the *mikoshi* is larger than the old one and,
in addition, with the growth in population since the end of
the war and the increased income from the fishing of waters
to a certain extent neglected in the war years, extensions
have been built on to a number of houses, these projecting
over the already narrow paths.

The most interesting aspect of the annual spring festival of the island shrine is the age, forty-two, of the male parishioners who act as officiants, or servers, in this festival and serve for the whole of their forty-second year. The age of forty-two, as has been said, is for the male the worst of the *yakudoshi*, the evil or critical years. It has been suggested that superstitions of this kind derive from the word-play of which the Japanese are so fond; *yaku* interpreted later as 'evil', was meant originally in its sense of 'service', the service of the *kami*. Contact with the *kami* in the course of such service put the server, his relatives and friends, and those of his age-group in the community in a potentially critical position in that some of the *kami*'s kamihood, his extraordinary or magic qualities, was almost inevitably transferred or reflected. Thus, the practice of service of the *kami* at the age of forty-two in the case of the males of this island that has always been reluctant to keep in contact with and change with outside influences, may well be a very valuable indication of the origin of this group of superstitions. This is one of a very small number of such instances so far known in the whole of Japan. (Incidentally, there is a grave shortage at the moment of men in the forty-two age group—those who never returned from the war, and there were many, would be at or approaching this age. For the past few years, to overcome this shortage, service at the island shrine has been extended to the forty-third year. This practice may be connected with the belief noted above that the evil of the 'evil' year extends to the preceding and following years.)

Of the remainder of the year-round ceremonies, the greater part are concerned with preparations for and the celebration of the New Year. On New Year's Eve, the islanders eat noodles to which a boiled fish-paste has been added; houses and boats are given a thorough cleaning since for the first days of the New Year no such work takes place. New Year's Day sees little more than visits to the homes of relatives—which must in itself be a highly complex manoeuvre when almost all the island's inhabitants are in some way inter-related. Okinoshima is like most rural communities in putting the greater emphasis on the Little New Year, centred on the January moon. On the evening of January 14th, *kadomatsu*, *shimenawa* and other New Year decorations are collected and made into two separate bonfire piles at the top of the harbour breakwater. The two fires are lit on Little New Year's Day—the ceremony is called *sagichō*—the larger by youths aged seventeen, the smaller by boys aged thirteen. In the case of the larger bonfire there is here, perhaps, a remnant of a part of the initiation ceremonies to mark the attainment of adulthood; the more elderly islanders still remember that in the January when a youth became seventeen, there was held a house ceremony to celebrate his entry into the Young Men's Group, his attainment of adulthood and the qualification of earning a wage. Rice-cakes toasted in the *sagichō* fires will ward off colds for the whole of the coming year and the ashes, strewn round the house, will keep off snakes. As elsewhere, these ashes are not used as agricultural or crop charms.

The rest of the year contains little celebration, for although retirement comes early and is withdrawal in its fullest sense, labours, or, more particularly, the tasks of fishing, are taken very seriously until the advent of the happy age. Okinoshima's fishermen only rest voluntarily on two days in the year, New Year's Day and May 9th; the remainder of the thirty or so days that are lost to fishing in an average year are the result of rest enforced by bad weather, by winds that make the lake too rough for fishing or endanger the boats' safety. Almost all Okinoshima's fishermen are out on the lake on three hundred and thirty days; of the rest of those who live by, or in part by, Lake Biwa's fish, a mere ten per cent fish on two hundred and seventy or more days in the year. There may well be a fairly intimate connection between the fishing seasons and the fact that the festivities which are celebrated most fully cluster about the New Year. The drag-net fishing season begins in April and lasts until late November, so that although the intervening period, December to March, is taken up by net fishing for roach, the fisherman, like the women farmers, is free of his heaviest labours at the New

Year. On the other hand, although the farmers may be in the midst of a fairly light period at the time of the spring festival, the season for drag-net fishing is at its height. In fact, the spring festival is timed to begin in the early afternoon, after the return of the co-operative boats, so that the festival day is not lost to fishing. Bon, which falls at a season when both farmers and fishermen are in the midst of heavy tasks, is given little heed.

On the day of the Boys' Festival, May 5th, two *chimaki*—rice cakes wrapped in bamboo leaves and rice straw—are hung by the lintel as a charm to ensure an unfailing supply of pocket money through the year. Bon is celebrated on August 24th, a strange departure from a date in the middle of the month when such great stress is put on the Little New Year. A month or so later comes the island deity's autumn festival. Early in December, with the end of the year's labours in the paddy, the new rice is eaten on the occasion of a great island feast. In contrast to wedding ceremonies, the men flock to this gathering, in spite of the fact that hardly one of them, except perhaps for the few hectic days of transplanting, has put his hand to a farming tool throughout the year.

There are several indications that Okinoshima's isolation and apartness are not to last so very much longer. For one thing, there seems to be a slight twinge of envy in the looks which the islanders direct at the quality of the clothes of the twenty-five or thirty exiles who come home each year—and nearly cause the tiny ferry boat to capsize—on the day of the spring festival. Nor is this merely because the exiles are wearing dress that is not home-made, for there is little tradition of home sewing on the island, another factor that sets it apart from almost every other rural community in Japan, where the sewing machine is an indispensable part of the bride's luggage. Almost the only item of home-made apparel on the island is the simple straw sandal, called elsewhere *waraji*, for which the more high-sounding term *zōri* here obstinately persists. A further pointer to a greater readiness to look outwards is the eagerness which the islanders have shown in registering their names for plots of land newly reclaimed from the lake on the mainland to the east, and the zest with which they tell you of their plans to reduce over-crowding in the tight island community and increase land holdings by establishing second sons and branch families across the water on the mainland.

Nor is this new sense of mobility merely outward looking. The plans of the parent church of the island's temples to build a holiday and recreation centre for Young Buddhists on the peak of the higher of the two hills in honour of the cele-brations in honour of Shinran's death, though at first received coldly, are now recognized as a means of bringing money and services to the island. The islanders, too, are spiriting their savings away to the mainland, investing in shares and in the larger banks in the mainland cities, much to the bewilder-ment of postmaster Nishii, who knows just about everything that is to be known about all their private lives and quite fails to understand the motive for their reluctance to pat-ronize his local Post Office Savings Bank!

Only in one aspect is the island more inward-looking than before. Until 1960, the young bloods always used their monthly trip to the barber in Hachiman City on the mainland as an excuse for a late night spree, a film and perhaps a meal and a drink out. But early in that year the island came to have its first barber, a young man whose hearing is failing rapidly and who has a blackboard in place of the usual mirror on which the customers write their 'Short back and sides please'. All that the young men can do nowadays is drop in at the larger of the general stores and watch television in the 'parlour' there for an hour on their way home after their haircut. Late-night, extra-mural revelling is now the sole privilege of the womenfolk, who, apart from the oldest of grandmothers, nearly all go for their regular two-monthly perm in Hachiman.

THE END